The Overachiever's Dilemma

The Overachiever's Dilemma

By CJ McClanahan

Printed in the United States of America

First Printing, 2017

ISBN 978-0-9986833-0-0 paperback

To my father Gary,
a great friend, cheerleader and inspirational mentor.

Contents

Introduction

I love to read.

I'm usually in the middle of two books at any one time and my office has multiple shelves filled with everything I've read since starting my business in 2003. I read book reviews, pay attention to what's in the *New York Times* or *Wall Street Journal* bestseller list and get a delivery from Amazon.com almost every other day.

Despite multiple attempts to engage in other interests, many years ago I came to the realization that reading is my only hobby. I've tried camping, fishing and even contemplated becoming a wine aficionado (until I realized that my pallet couldn't distinguish the difference between an $8 and $100 bottle of merlot). No matter what I've tried, nothing can keep my interest as much as a good book.

I focus almost exclusively on non-fiction (although I do love Vince Flynn, Clive Cussler and Dan Brown) and seem to gravitate towards the following genres: personal development, spiritual, psychology, business and current events.

I have a great deal of admiration for the author who can quickly grab my attention and compose such an interesting story that I get lost in their words for hours. Some of my favorite authors with this ability include Brene Brown, Donald Miller, Michael Lewis and Malcolm Gladwell.

In addition, because I love learning, I'm drawn to books that promise to deliver insight on interesting subjects backed by truckloads of data. Their lessons challenge my thinking and introduce me to ideas and concepts that I would have never considered on my own. These authors influence the way I run my business, parent my kids and take care of my health. I got hooked on this type of approach many years ago when I read *Talent is Overrated* by Geoff Colvin.

Lastly, I'm equally captivated by the authors whose words are so bold and powerful they seem to grab me by the shoulders, shake me vigorously until I've heard the message loud and clear. These books are shorter and don't waste time with text that isn't necessary to drive home the point. I've found a few that I really enjoy, including Rob Bell and Steven Pressfield.

Despite the fact that I love reading, every now and then I run across a book that I struggle to enjoy and often quit before I reach the end. I don't put these on my bookshelves because I have this somewhat irrational belief that they don't deserve a spot in my office if they weren't good enough to complete. I know it's silly.

The type of books that usually get this treatment typically have a handful of similar qualities. First, they're usually written by a PhD who is crazy smart and has spent years researching the subject. Unfortunately, despite their intellect, they struggle to write in a fashion that anyone (other than another PhD) would enjoy. Worst of all, these books are really long because the author feels compelled to detail the forty-three experiments necessary to justify each and every idea presented.

I wouldn't call these terrible books or even bad authors - I simply don't find them compelling. I believe that unless you're blessed with the rare ability to write so beautifully that the reader doesn't even care what the book is about (Malcom Gladwell, Michael Lewis, etc.) then I'd rather you get to the point in as few words as possible.

My taste in books is a direct reflection of my personality. Because I haven't been blessed with the ability (or the patience) to paint a beautiful picture with every sentence that comes out of my mouth, I tend to get right to the point. I quickly analyze a situation, build a logical case and deliver my recommendation with as little fluff as possible.

This style has its pros and cons. From a professional perspective, it's allowed me to be an effective leader and help hundreds of executives make substantial progress in their businesses. Personally, this approach could use some softening when it comes to discussions with my wife or disciplining the children. In addition, I'm not everyone's favorite non-profit board member – it's not unusual for me to sit quietly in a meeting until the very end when I declare, "I've listened to all the information, now here's what we're going to do."

I'm not trying to make the argument that my method is the most effective. Nor am I always proud of the results it generates. But over the years, I've gotten comfortable with who I am and recognize that this is the way I communicate, including the way I write.

This next 141 pages contain a straightforward plan for figuring out how to get more satisfaction from all your hard work. I could have added hundreds of pages filled with further evidence supporting my ideas, but as I mentioned, I'm not big on fluff. My goal isn't to wow you with words; I'm committed to inspire you to change behavior. The last thing you need is another book on your shelf whose advice you ignore.

The conclusions I reach and guidance provided are based on my personal and professional experience. I've had quite a journey filled with a bunch of triumphs and some really big mistakes. Most importantly, this advice is based on the 10,000+ hours I've spent coaching hundreds of overachieving professionals.

In other words, I know exactly how you're feeling and I take this opportunity to join you on this journey very seriously. If you take the time to slowly read this book and complete the short exercises at the end of each chapter, I *guarantee* you'll experience a paradigm shift that will change the way you feel about your personal and professional accomplishments.

The Chase

> "God gives one person riches, wealth, and honor so that he doesn't lack anything he wants. Yet, God doesn't give him the power to enjoy any of them. Instead, a stranger enjoys them. This is pointless and is a painful tragedy."
>
> – Ecclesiastes 6:2

Jeremy had it good.

At the young age of 42, he'd accomplished more than he ever thought possible. He was the top-producing partner at one of the most prestigious law firms in the Midwest and his salary over the last 3 years averaged more than $500,000. He was married to his college sweetheart and blessed with two beautiful children. His 6,000 square foot home overlooked the 13th green at the most exclusive golf club, where he played nine holes every weekend. He drove a cherry red BMW 5 Series and just purchased his wife a new Escalade with the Platinum package. Vacations were spent at luxurious far-away locales, each one a little bit nicer than the last. Best of all, he had a morning ritual that made him feel on top of the world every day: he would strap on one of his seven Breitling watches, relishing the feeling of the $5,000 timepiece on his wrist. It was to him, the ultimate sign of success.

None of this achievement came easy.

Jeremy worked sixty hours a week and rarely made it home before the kids went to bed. He justified the long hours by insisting that he could dial it back as soon as he made senior partner. He felt *so close* to having everything he needed to enjoy complete happiness and satisfaction. "Just a little bit more," he kept promising himself and his family.

But in the meantime, there was another side to his story. He believed he had to be vigilant because his firm was full of overachievers who were all intent on doing whatever it took to take his position as the top performer in the office. The wolves were *after* him, and at any moment, they could bring him down. So he couldn't let up, he couldn't give them an inch. He *had* to keep working hard.

Jeremy was feeling a similar pressure to keep up with his neighbors. Two of them had recently purchased summer homes on the lake and he seemed to find himself in never-ending conversations about the furniture, boats, and "man caves" each was building. Jeremy added "summer home" as a new milestone he needed to reach to keep up with everyone else. Once he got *that*, he could back off.

As the pressure mounted, he found it more and more difficult to deal with the stress. During the day, it was all smiles, meetings and closing big deals. But at night, Jeremy felt overwhelmed with all the demands on his time, and alcohol seemed to be the only thing that could help him relax. Eventually, he needed at least three glasses of Merlot to take the edge off so he could fall asleep before the alarm sounded at 5:15 am, beginning the cycle all over again.

Shortly before his 44th birthday all the hard work paid off and Jeremy was named senior partner at the firm. This promotion included a significant increase in compensation and more importantly, recognition as one of the most influential leaders within the entire legal community.

After celebrating with his partners, Jeremey scheduled a spontaneous weekend trip to New York City with his wife, Sarah. During their first night on the town, he slipped the hostess $100 to get a table at one of the city's hippest restaurants. With a chilled glass of Dom Perignon 2002 firmly in hand, he laughed and said, "I finally made it!" He and Sarah spent much of the weekend relaxing and discussing how much fun it would be to live a "normal" lifestyle, where they could finally take advantage of all the things they hadn't done through the years because Jeremy was always working or at the office.

When they returned home, Jeremy dialed back his workload, grilled burgers or steak almost every night, and even took a few Friday afternoons off to take the kids to the pool. He and Sarah started planning weekend outings and long vacations. His family was thrilled that he was so engaged with them. Life was good.

But, then "it" happened.

At the next partners meeting, Jeremy noticed that there were at least a half dozen of his peers who generated significantly more billings than he had in the last quarter. Despite the fact that he likely had a guaranteed salary of at least $600,000 for the next 20 years, he noticed a knot in his stomach when these results were distributed to the group.

He felt ashamed and embarrassed.

The next week, Jeremy spent the majority of his waking hours beating himself up over his lack of production. He believed that his results were completely unacceptable, and committed himself to doing whatever it took to regain his title as an elite performer. This refocus worked and in less than a year his revenue numbers were once again near the top.

Jeremy was committed to keeping them there. He would do anything to avoid the shame he felt at that partners meeting. He had never been mediocre and he wasn't about to start now.

The next eight years were virtually identical to his first twenty in the firm. He outworked just about everyone and was routinely recognized, and compensated, as one of the most valuable members in his office. He got that summer home on the lake, the boat, the man cave. He'd firmly cemented his position at the top of the mountain and wasn't coming down for anything or anyone.

The only difference between those eight years and the twenty that came before them was the increased levels of stress and anxiety. Jeremy struggled to find time for activities that didn't relate to work, missing his kid's sporting events, school activities, and anniversaries. His sporadic vacations were filled with conference calls and hours in front of his laptop. At the age of 52, Jeremy had resigned himself to the fact that this lifestyle was the price you had to pay to be recognized as the best in his industry. "That's just the way it is," he told himself.

Then, one summer, Jeremy realized his kids were nearing the age when they start thinking about college and leaving home. Time was running out – so he booked a ten-day cruise to the Virgin Islands, and announced the trip to his family. But instead of being thrilled, both of his children – now teenagers – grumbled at the news. They didn't want to miss their friends and a bunch of summer activities.

Jeremy was furious. He vented to Sarah: "What in the hell is wrong with these kids?" Instead of responding with empathy, Sarah looked her husband right in the eye and delivered the painful truth: "You've put your career in front of the kids since they were born and they barely know you. Did you think that you could just dive back into their lives with a fancy vacation and they'd jump for joy? You made your bed and now it's time to sleep in it."

In this moment, Jeremy's heart sank and he finally saw what he had sacrificed. He realized that he had no idea what success really meant.

The Success Formula

Like Jeremy, most overachieving professionals (yes, I'm talking to you) allow this simple definition of success to guide just about every decision they make:

Tons of Effort = Lots of Achievement = Happiness/Satisfaction

Following this equation since middle school has probably served you well. Unfortunately, there's just one tiny glitch in the equation. For some reason, regardless of the size of the achievement, the "happiness" and "satisfaction" you're supposed to be enjoying only lasts for a short periods of time – sometime only *hours*.

Up until now, you assumed these periods of satisfaction would grow over time and you convinced yourself that deep lasting joy was certain to occur as soon as you made partner, got promoted to Vice President, or hit the million dollar mark in sales.

Unfortunately, it's not working out that way. That's why you picked up this book.

You're wondering why life feels like a non-stop parade of accomplishments, each one greater than the last, but none delivering any lasting satisfaction. You're beginning to doubt the accuracy of the success formula you've followed diligently for years. You're wondering if all the effort is worth the infrequent, fleeting glimpses of contentment. You're hoping there's more to life than non-stop activity that's filled with stress, anxiety and worry.

You're Not Alone

One of the more frustrating aspects of this doubt is that from the outside you appear to be the only one struggling with these issues. Your next-door neighbor just bought a boat and seems happier than ever. Your college roommate received another promotion and is taking his family to Hawaii to celebrate. Your brother-in-law was recently named one of the most influential cardiologists in the country and never seems to have a bad day.

Everyone else appears to have figured out how to achieve their dreams while enjoying the associated happiness and satisfaction. You assume they're all "normal" and *you're* the one with the psychological issues. You're the one who constantly feels unsatisfied.

Don't be so tough on yourself.

If thirteen years coaching hundreds of professionals has taught me anything, it's that you're not alone. There are millions of overachievers struggling with these same questions, wondering if there's a better way. Trust me, your neighbor, college roommate and brother-in-law are worried about exactly the same things you are, and feeling exactly the same emotions. It's just that none of them are talking about it.

What's going on? Why in an age of abundance, where most professionals experience more prosperity than at any other time in human history, are so many unsatisfied with their accomplishments?

I've spent the last ten years exploring this question and I've got a theory. My research and 10,000+ hours coaching hundreds of professionals has illustrated a consistent pattern. While attempting to follow the classic success formula (*Tons of Work = Lots of Achievement = Happiness and Success*), most overachievers get caught up in an unintended cycle that typically leads to increased stress and less fulfillment. Instead of a straight line, their path gets warped and ends up looking like this:

Tons of Effort

Lots of Achievement

New Shortcomings

The "Overachiever's Trap"

The first piece of the sequence produces the intended result –

tons of effort (studying, work, etc.) leads to lots of achievement (straight A's, promotion at the office, etc.). Unfortunately, shortly after the accomplishment (sometimes within hours), instead of enjoying the triumph, most overachievers shift their focus towards what needs to be done next, i.e. their shortcomings.

Tell me if this sounds familiar. You just landed a great new promotion at your firm and a few weeks later, as you're packing up to leave for the night, you notice a peer is still in the office. This guy is on an identical career track and the last thing you want is for the boss to see him working later than you. So, you unpack your laptop, return to your office (door open and light on - you want to make sure everyone notices you're still there) and get back to it.

Don't be ashamed, we've all done it.

Shortly after starting my coaching business back in 2003, I was named one of the top "rookies" in the nation. I loved this recognition and expected to savor the achievement for at least the remainder of the year. I distinctly remember enjoying the award for about a week and then quickly shifting my sights towards the next goal. A few months later, I landed a coveted board position and again assumed I could sit back and enjoy my hard work. But, as you can probably guess – I didn't. This cycle continued for years.

In both cases, the hard work led to a great achievement. But, instead of slowing down to really enjoy the feeling of satisfaction, my mind refocused on the required "lots of effort" to achieve the *next* accomplishment. In many cases the overachiever's brain becomes *addicted* to success and like any addiction, the next fix (i.e. achievement) needs to be bigger than the last to produce the necessary "high."

The cycle never ends – it just gets faster and faster. You've gotten yourself on a treadmill that isn't going to stop anytime soon – and that is the dilemma facing every overachieving professional. Do you continue to work yourself to death in an effort to attain endless professional achievements? Or, do you slow down, rethink your approach, and consider looking elsewhere for happiness and satisfaction?

It's an extremely tough question, one which we're going to explore in detail over the next 132 pages. Before we do, I think it's important to examine a foundational issue: what causes someone to develop an unhealthy obsession with success in the first place?

Early Programming

I may not have any idea if Indiana will ever win another national championship, but there's one thing I do know with absolute certainty: at no point in your life did you ever utter the following phrase: "I'd love to develop a belief system that keeps me from fully enjoying my life!"

Your upbringing was likely filled with parents, teachers, coaches and friends who did the absolute very best they could with the resources at their disposal. They worked hard to provide you with the type of guidance that would lead to a happy and successful life. None of these individuals, not one, wanted you to develop an unhealthy mindset by the time you became an adult.

Yet, despite everyone's best efforts and intentions, you've somehow become an overachieving professional who struggles to fully enjoy the benefits of all your hard work.

This begs the question – *How did you, me, and millions of others get this way?*

There are many factors at play, but a fundamental truth is that we begin to focus on being "successful" at a very young age. Consider this story about a recent visit I made to my daughter's third grade class.

I was asked to deliver the standard "*What does my dad do for a living?*" talk. After providing an overview of my business, I opened it up for questions. A bunch of hands shot up and I selected a boy in the back who confidently asked, "How much money do you make?"

Surprised with the inquiry, I stammered a little before I got out, "Just enough." Unsatisfied, he followed up with "How much is that?" I deflected again, but next, a young girl asked, "How much do you get paid every time you speak?" Again, a little amazed, I replied that it depended on the size of the group and the topic.

"Is it more than $100?" shouted out another student and before I could answer, I heard, "How about $500?" from the other side of the room.

For the first time in my career, I was speechless in front of an audience. Luckily, Mrs. Street brought the "auction" to a close and asked the class to thank me for the visit. I left the room stunned by the unapologetic grilling I received from a room full of nine-year-olds.

After some reflection, I understood what happened in Mrs. Street's classroom that afternoon. These young people were sizing me up, because at some level they wanted to know if I was successful. In their little third grade minds, they assumed that the best way to measure the success of a parent is to figure out how much money they make. Which made me wonder the following: why does a nine-year-old care so much about success? How did they decide that income was the best measurement? And most importantly, at what age does this focus begin?

"Money is a source of mystery to children," says Ron Lieber, author of *The Opposite of Spoiled: Raising Kids Who Are Grounded, Generous, and Smart About Money*, in an article in the New York Times.[i] "They sense its power, so they ask questions, lots of them, over many years. Why isn't our house as big as my cousin's? Why can't I have a carnivorous plant terrarium? Why should I respect my teachers if they earn only $60,000 per year? (Real question!) Are we poor?"

You can see how kids become programmed from any early age to believe that the only way to feel satisfaction/happiness in life is to constantly chase success, and that success is defined from the start as "out-achieving our peers in every way possible."

We can't do a damn thing about the environment we grew up in. Most psychologists agree that your experiences as a child heavily influence the types of behavior you'll demonstrate later in life. Additionally, research also indicates that your brain isn't fully developed until your mid-twenties. As a result, from birth until 25-ish, our brains absorb millions of bits of information from our environment. We take this information and develop a "program" that helps interpret our happiness and satisfaction for the rest of our lives. Most importantly, we didn't consciously

---

i   Ron Lieber, "Why You Should Tell Your Kids How Much You Make," *New York Times*, February 1, 2015, BU1.

choose most of the data that makes such an influential impact in the person we become.

Consider an example of the typical upbringing for an over-achieving professional. Let's call him CJ – imagine him being 6'5" and really good looking. As early as he can remember (Mrs. Webber's third grade class), CJ was rewarded with praise for getting good grades in school. Soon, the term "gifted" and "bright" were used when describing his abilities. Eventually, this lead to a spot in the advanced class with the other "special" kids. CJ, remember, was smart: he noticed that he received additional praise from his parents and teachers every time he earned the best grades or any other accolades.

Quickly, CJ noticed this link between hard work, achievement and positive feedback from parents and teachers. Because this praise felt good, he continued doing whatever it took to earn more. Before too long, CJ was labeled an overachiever – an identity he eagerly embraced. At this time, he also began to judge others by how well they did both inside the classroom (grades) and outside (sports, friends, etc.).

Soon, CJ found himself surrounded by friends who shared his commitment to hard work and achievement. It was like he joined a club that was full of people who were more "gifted" than everyone else. He and his fellow overachievers spent the majority of their days competing to be recognized as the "best." CJ couldn't imagine being considered average. Every new accomplishment (Honor Roll, straight A's, winning the science fair, etc.) continued to be met with compliments and accolades.

As the accomplishments piled up, CJ's brain became programmed to *need* the affirmations and praise from others to just feel normal. After completing middle school, this programming turned into an obsession.

Like most overachievers, CJ found high school to be a little more challenging. The quality of competition jumped considerably and there were more opportunities (National Honor Society, athletics, etc.) to compare himself to everyone else and ultimately to measure *his* "worth." He continued to work his butt off to ensure he earned the appropriate praise and began to look ahead to the most important appreciation of his efforts up to this point in his young life: acceptance to a great college program.

College turned out to be a non-stop competition for grades and extra-curricular activities.

CJ, of course, worked tirelessly. However, college courses weren't easy and he had to outstudy everyone else to earn a B+ average. Because he struggled to flourish in the classroom, CJ had to look for other ways to stay even with his fellow overachievers. He did this by getting involved in just about every extracurricular activity he could find. These efforts fulfilled his overachiever cravings and he was eventually rewarded for all his hard work. By the end of his senior year, CJ was named to the Indiana University Homecoming Court and recognized as the top student leader in the country for his fraternity. He even graduated in the top 10% of his class, and began to look ahead to how he could outperform everybody else in his chosen career.

Even though your upbringing might not mirror mine in every way, I'm sure you notice similarities. You probably got good grades and hung out with a group of high achievers. You compared accomplishments throughout middle/high school as you competed to get into the best college. You relished the praise from your teachers, parents and coaches every time you reached another goal. After a certain level of achievement, you began to feel that you were part of a "special" group that was better than the rest.

However, at no point did either of us say, "I am going to choose to become the type of person who is never satisfied unless I am outdoing everyone else and recognized as a top performer." I seriously doubt that any of your family members, teachers or coaches ever said to you, "Unless you're in the top 1% of everything you do, your life will be shit." It was simply a message we absorbed from our environment, and after 20+ years on this planet, we were convinced that overachieving was the *only* way to find happiness.

Turning the Page

In 2007, after I had been coaching business executives for almost five years, I began to notice something interesting. I had a handful of clients who were making significant progress and really crushing it. They were earning more than at any time in their lives and there seemed to be no end in sight to what they could achieve. I was pleased about their progress, and began to think about how I could get my other clients up to their speed, but what I noticed was that despite their off-the-charts success, these were some of my least satisfied clients. No matter how much they achieved, they always wanted more. It was never enough.

As my practice grew, I noticed that more and more of my clients suffered from the same affliction. They had gotten caught up in the same "overachievers trap" I had been cycling through for the majority of my adult life.

It was at this point that I asked myself *the* question: "Is all this success worth the effort if you don't appreciate the journey?" The answer I came to was a resounding "no." No amount of achievement is *ever* a worthwhile tradeoff for a lifetime of frustration. None, zero, nada.

My epiphany led to the understanding that something profound needed to change. I needed to rethink how I lived my life, raised my children and coached the executives I worked with each day – and I did.

Since then, I've turned my efforts to helping overachieving professionals understand the overachiever's dilemma, and solve it. I help them continue to achieve big goals *while at the same time* reducing stress and enjoying their accomplishments. After more than ten years of effort, research and experimentation, I'm excited to roll out a system that I've seen work time and time again.

In the next six chapters, I'm going introduce powerful strategies for the overachieving professional that can change your life. This process addresses fundamental concepts, each one building out a framework for making *lasting* changes in your behavior.

- *How Should I Define Success?* Every decision you make is heavily influenced by whether or not the behavior will drive you toward, or away from, success. As a result, before you try and improve anything, you need to first revise your definition. This chapter will provide you with an effective definition that will shape your daily behavior.

- *What Makes Me Unique?* Most overachieving professionals assume that with enough effort they can be good at everything. Not only is this premise false, striving to do something you don't enjoy and doesn't come naturally is zero fun. I'll help you identify your unique talents and figure out how to inject these skills into your professional life.

- *Why are Meaningful Relationships so Important?* A funny thing happened on my journey to learn about satisfaction and happiness. I discovered that it's virtually impossible to be happy without positive relationships with the people you love. This section is dedicated to helping you prioritize building your personal and professional relationships without giving up the corner office.

- *What's the Best Way to Enjoy the Journey?* Once you understand these first four strategies, you'll have the footings of a strong foundation for living a more satisfying life. However, you will still face difficult challenges along the way. This chapter will detail the proven tactics for overcoming these challenges and appreciating the journey.

So here you sit, about to embark on a journey that will challenge most of the assumptions upon which you've built a very successful life. At the very least, the next 125 pages will change your perspective about what it means to be successful. If you let them, these lessons will profoundly change your life.

But all I can really do is teach you the best practices I've learned over the last ten years. Like all good books, the best these words can possibly accomplish is to inspire you to change your behavior. You're going to have to do the hard work.

From one overachieving professional to another, I know you're up for the challenge.

<u>**Three Key Points to Remember**</u>

1. Most overachievers are following the following definition/model for success because it predictably leads to a jammed resume, a bunch of recognition and a high salary. ***Tons of Effort = Lots of Achievement = Happiness/Satisfaction***

2. Millions of overachievers now know that this process rarely leads to the type of contentment they're hoping to find. The reason is that instead of being a straight line, this approach actually turns into a vicious circle called the Overachiever's Trap. No matter how hard we work, it's nearly impossible to break free.

Tons of Effort

Lots of Achievement

New Shortcomings

3. You were wired from an early age to believe that constantly outdoing as many of your peers as possible was the only way to feel successful. You didn't wake up one day and consciously decide: "I'd like my life to be filled with tons of stress and never truly feel satisfied with my achievements." This wiring didn't happen overnight and it will take some time to reprogram your way of thinking – but it's very doable.

Take Action

One of my favorite quotes comes from the bestselling author Stephen Covey: "*To know and not to do is really not to know.*" In other words, you might as well stop reading this book if you're not going to do something with what you've learned.

Learning isn't really all that hard. As soon as the internet became ubiquitous, finding the answers to even our most difficult questions became easy. Doing something with this information – now that's another story. We've all read a great book, attended a seminar or watched what we assumed would be a "life changing" documentary only to completely forget everything we'd learned forty-eight hours later.

As a result, at the end of every chapter, I've designed a short exercise (15-20 minutes) that will force you to stop, think about what you've just read and take some action. Believe it or not, this small amount of effort can really make a huge difference in helping you to make a lasting change in behavior.

Chapter 1 – Taking Action

As an overachiever, at each stage in your life you set ambitious goals and worked hard to achieve them. This first exercise is designed to help you examine how you've enjoyed your efforts over the years.

1. Fill out each column utilizing the following as a guideline:

- Success – Reflect back on your life from middle school until today. During each period list an achievement that at the time you were absolutely certain would make you feel extremely successful. For example:

    o Middle School – Make the football team.

    o High School – Get accepted to Harvard

    o 22 – 30 Years – Earn $100,000+

    o 30 – 40 Years – Make partner

    o 40 – 50 Years – Buy a lake house

    o 50 + Years – Become CEO

- Enjoyment – Next, take a guess at how long you remember actually enjoying the achievement before you recognized it wasn't enough and needed to accomplish something else to truly feel successful. Was it a day, a week, a month?

2. Finally, list 1-3 goals you're striving to achieve today that you believe are the key to delivering your happiness and satisfaction. Once this is complete, look back at this exercise and ask yourself the following question: "What am I actually working so hard to achieve?"

You can complete the exercise below or by downloading a template at CoachCJ.com/bookexercises.

Age?	Success?	Enjoyment?
Middle School		
High School		
College		
22 – 30 years		
30 – 40 years		
40 – 50 years		
50 years +		

	Goal/Objective
1	
2	
3	

CHAPTER 2

Paradigm Shift

"When you change the way you look at things, the things you look at change."

— Wayne Dyer

We are all a product of our times – and we tend to believe what others around us believe.

If you lived back in the fourth century BC, for example, there was one thing most highly regarded intellectuals agreed on: the earth was at the center of the universe. Everything else – the sun, the moon and the other planets – revolved around the current world. This was known as the "geocentric model," and was so highly regarded that two of Greece's most influential philosophers, Plato and Aristotle, wrote works based on the theory. In the second century BC, this concept became officially formalized by the astronomer Claudius Ptolemy, and was held as absolute truth for more than 1200 years. In 1000 AD a handful of astronomers, scientists and philosophers began to challenge the ideas – among them, Copernicus and then Newton – and gradually, the firmly held paradigm changed completely. By the end of the seventeenth century, it became clear that the Earth was one of a handful of planets that revolved around a star we call the sun and that ours was just one of millions of these systems throughout the universe. This change in understanding is known as a *paradigm shift* – a complete shift in the way people see the whole world – and it gives context to what we are going to talk about in relation to your view of success.

Like the people living in the time of Aristotle and Copernicus, you live your life according to a set of paradigms: beliefs and assumptions that guide the way you construe your environment. You have strong beliefs about thousands of topics, including religion, politics, parenting and global warming. Each of your paradigms shapes your perspective and the way you interpret information on these issues.

Paradigms are very powerful and typically extremely hard to break. Once we develop a strong view on a subject, we tend to find ourselves drawn to information (newspaper articles, TV shows and blogs) that reinforce our belief. This approach creates an "echo chamber" and keeps us from considering any data that doesn't support our viewpoint. It's the reason Fox News and MSNBC are so popular.

It's also the reason that you find yourself with such a dilemma as an overachieving professional. As we discussed in the first chapter, you've followed a paradigm since you were young, which is based on a belief that this is the best formula for defining success:

Tons of Effort = Lots of Achievement and Recognition = Happiness/Satisfaction

This paradigm was reinforced by your teachers, parents, friends, coaches, managers, mentors and by virtually every news source in your environment. In your echo chamber, all you kept hearing was: *"The only way to be successful is to keep outworking everyone else."* Before you can address the challenges you're facing and improve your quality of life, you'll need to first examine this paradigm, and change this belief system. If you don't adjust the way you define success, you'll find it impossible to make any meaningful progress and feel satisfied with your efforts.

Sounds easy, but I know from experience that this is an extremely difficult paradigm to break. It's easier to convince a Yankees fan to root for the Red Sox than it is to persuade an overachieving professional to stop using income, job title, size of house, type of car, etc., as the most important measurements of success.

There's a reason it's so hard. You've become addicted to the feeling that's associated with achievement and the accompanying recognition. Every time you "win" at something you get a hit of dopamine in your brain – a neurotransmitter that influences the way you feel. Because you enjoy this sensation, you do whatever it takes to feel this way. This obsession with success is no different than any other addiction – it's unhealthy and always leads to disappointment.

Consider the story of a typical drug addict. They start off using in recreational settings. Soon, they realize how much better they feel when using and begin taking the drug on a more regular basis. Eventually, they develop a tolerance and need a larger dose each time to feel the same "high." The next thing you know, they are addicted, and if they can't get a fix, they experience severe withdrawal symptoms. They begin to organize their entire lives around the next fix, sacrificing money, time, relationship, health and everything else to the next high.

Now, think about how this compares to the overachieving professional: you. In the beginning, all you needed was a regular compliment from the boss, a small annual raise and a few new clients to feel satisfied with the progress of your career. Unfortunately, like being hooked on heroin, you soon built up a tolerance to this type of recognition. These kinds of achievements were suddenly no longer enough to make you happy – you needed more. Today, you might need to be the highest paid member of your firm, the top ranked salesperson in the region, or even the CEO to feel any fulfillment at all. The cartoon below[ii] clearly illustrates your current dilemma. You can run as fast as you want, but the carrots just keep getting bigger, and they will always be just out of your grasp.

---

ii   Dave Carpenter, Cartoon Stock, https://www.cartoonstock.com/directory/k/karat.asp.

You can keep doing it the way you were taught, which will probably lead to a ton of cultural success (money, recognition, acquisitions), but very little happiness or satisfaction. Or, you can change your paradigm and try a new approach. This starts with you rethinking your definition of success.

Does this mean I'm going to spend the rest of this book criticizing your lifestyle, then suggesting that you quit your job, sell your house, give away all your worldly belongings and join the Peace Corps? I give you my word that the answer to this question is a resounding "no" (unless, of course, you want to join the Peace Corps which is an amazing organization doing great work). This book is about changing your perspective, reducing your stress, and getting more satisfaction from your life. This can be done while living in a big house, going on great vacations and working in the corner office. It's more of a "both/and" as opposed to "either/or."

Success 2.0

As I mentioned in Chapter One, I was brought up believing that overachievement leads to happiness. I embraced this paradigm and, like you, struggled to find satisfaction in all the hard work. I achieved a ton, felt a hit of happiness, and then had to re-up to achieve even more to feel it again. It wasn't until I had been coaching overachieving professionals for about five years that I started to question our shared definition of success and the constant drive to accomplish more. I began to wonder if all of this hard work was worth the recognition and achievements if no one ever really enjoyed the journey. And by no one, I meant myself, many of my friends, and the majority of my clients. I decided to see if there was a better definition.

I launched my search by re-evaluating the belief system we'd all held since the third grade – the one that holds that *Tons of Effort = Lots of Achievement and Recognition = Happiness/Satisfaction.*

I carefully analyzed my entire life to determine if I could spot a theme or identify any trends related to that equation. I looked back year after year and wrote down every BIG accomplishment that I achieved and then noted how long it took before I was on to the next objective. At times it seemed like I would only enjoy the achievement for a few hours before I crossed it off a mental list and it was no longer that big a deal. It became clear that while the hard work did predictably lead to achievement, the happiness was always short-lived, and just like an addict, I needed more recognition each time to feel any satisfaction at all.

Next, I decided to study my coaching clients – most of them overachieving professionals – to see if their experiences were similar to mine. Almost to a man/woman I found them to be identical. They all ended up feeling restless, unsure, and needing a bigger "win" to feel good about themselves. No matter what they achieved, it never seemed to be enough for them to feel happy and fulfilled.

For example, I once had a client that increased his/her personal income by more than 50% and barely even noticed because of his/her obsession with a peer who had done even better. That same year, just a few days after his/her team blew past their revenue targets, one of my clients decided to ignore the accomplishment and instead sent out a terse email to the whole leadership team warning them not to become complacent.

After reflecting on my life and the experiences of dozens of professionals, I was now certain that my current success paradigm was indeed flawed and needed to be reexamined. Money, recognition and acquisitions don't buy you happiness.

I explored a variety of different approaches for describing success to try to figure out how to break the paradigm. I read dozens of books on the subject, attended workshops, listened to motivational speakers and of course spent a great deal of time on Google, which allowed me to quickly learn what some of history's most influential thinkers had to say about the topic. As you can imagine, it's possible to find an unlimited number of different opinions surrounding the idea of what it means to be successful. I found a handful of classic schools of thought regarding this concept.

Hard Work – This sentiment infers that success is directly related to the amount of effort you put towards any endeavor.

- *"I do not know anyone who has got to the top without hard work. That is the recipe. It will not always get you to the top, but should get you pretty near."* – Margaret Thatcher, Prime Minister of the UK from 1979 – 1990

- *"Talent is cheaper than table salt. What separates the talented individual from the successful one is a lot of hard work."* – Stephen King, Author

Perseverance – This opinion reflects the importance of bouncing back from failure.

- *"Success is how high you bounce when you hit bottom."* – George S. Patton, U.S. Army General during WWII

- *"I do not think that there is any other quality so essential to success of any kind as the quality of perseverance. It overcomes almost everything, even nature."* – John D. Rockefeller, American Oil Industry Tycoon

Making a difference – The idea is that success is directly related to what you give back to the world.

- *"I have one life and one chance to make it count for something... My faith demands that I do whatever I can, wherever I am, whenever I can, for as long as I can with whatever I have to try to make a difference."* – Jimmy Carter, 39th President of the United States

- *"From what we get, we can make a living; what we give, however, makes a life."* – Arthur Ashe, Former #1 tennis player in the world

Doing Your Best – Some argue that success is how much you get out of the talents you've been given.

- *"The man who has done his best has done everything."* – Charles Schwab, American businessman who pioneered the discount sales of Wall Street securities

- *"The difference between what we do and what we are capable of doing would suffice to solve most of the world's problems."* – Albert Einstein, Theoretical Physicist who developed the Theory of Relativity

After completing this research, I found each one of these concepts extremely compelling. Working hard, persevering, giving back and doing your best (in addition to many other sentiments I'm sure I missed) are all important ingredients of success. But, I still felt that something was missing. I felt the need to continue researching, brainstorming and wordsmithing to put together a definition of success that would make sense to the overachieving professional.

It wasn't easy, but after months of trial and error, I developed a description that I am confident is applicable to everyone, and *especially* meaningful to the overachieving professional. This simple statement is the result of thirteen years of coaching hundreds of professionals, dozens of workshops, a boatload of webinars and a library full of more than three hundred personal development/ business books. Here goes:

Success is… The extent to which I utilize my unique abilities, build meaningful relationships and enjoy the journey.

I'll spend the remainder of this chapter detailing why these sixteen words represent a powerful definition for the professional who struggles to feel successful despite a jam-packed resume full of accomplishments and accolades.

Discover Your Unique Abilities

As I mentioned, I believe that there's value in each of the schools of thought regarding the meaning of success. However, I feel that the overachieving professional needs to start their definition by first focusing on what makes them different from everyone else. Specifically, what are their unique skills, what comes easy, and what do they enjoy doing the most? Albert Schweitzer captured my intent perfectly when he said, "Success is not the key to happiness. Happiness is the key to success. If you love what you are doing, you will be successful."

What struck me is how different this is from the experience of most overachieving professionals. We are herded by our schools into job placement programs where we often take the job that seems the most prestigious and offers the biggest economic upside, because we have been trained to measure success in this way. The next thing you know, we are "successful" professionals but we are stuck in a career we don't enjoy because our lifestyle and self-esteem has become tied directly to our job title.

If you want the satisfaction and happiness that success promises, you'll want to spend as much of your life as possible doing something that's a good fit with your unique skills, abilities and personality. This concept has been studied by many experts who focus on human fulfillment, happiness and creativity. In his book *Flow*, Mihaly Csikszentmihalyi examines what happens when someone is involved in an activity to which they are uniquely suited. He explained to Wired® magazine the state of flow as "being completely involved in an activity for its own sake. The ego falls away. Time flies. Every action, movement, and thought follows inevitably from the previous one, like playing jazz. Your whole being is involved, and you're using your skills to the utmost."

We all have probably had a taste of what that was like – maybe when you were lost in jamming on a guitar, deep in the fourth quarter of a big game, or even falling in love. Flow often characterizes our happiest moments in life. So why not bring that concept to the definition of success? In other words, do what you love the most, which best utilizes your unique skills, and you'll get a ton of joy out of life.

This makes sense, because it means that success comes in many shapes, sizes and flavors. Success is not limited to the top 1% just because they've chosen a professional path that includes a big salary. A school teacher,[iii] social worker or mailman can feel the type of success that is theoretically enjoyed by the CEO of a Fortune 500 company, and we all know that this is logical and true. If success is ever going to bring you satisfaction, it needs to be linked to what drives you – not what the world insists is important.

The idea that everyone is designed with their own unique abilities was very relevant to my own professional journey. After five or six years in the coaching business I was determined to grow a company that would rival some of the largest in the local marketplace. I began developing new services, hiring staff and thinking "bigger." I soon discovered that the more complex the business became, the less I enjoyed it. I found myself spending the majority of my time managing moving parts and less time inspiring professionals, which is what I enjoyed doing the most.

Initially, I was frustrated and a little upset that I didn't "have what it takes" to be the market leader in my industry. I was envious of a handful of my peers who'd taken the big risks, grew large staffs and attracted significantly more recognition and clients than myself. This envy and frustration kept me from feeling successful with my own business. I'd convinced myself that I was viewed as a "second tier" performer in the marketplace and wouldn't ever be recognized as a leader in my field. At times, I even began to question if I'd chosen the wrong profession.

But, over time my perspective changed. I began to get more

---

iii   I have two young kids (10 and 13) and there are few people more important to their development than the teachers who mentor them seven hours a day, nine months out of the year. If inspiring the next generation isn't important, then nothing is.

comfortable in my own skin and recognized that it was okay to run a business that was the best fit for my unique skills, abilities and disposition. I realized that I wasn't giving up on going big because the task was too hard. I was intentionally making a conscious choice to build a company that I would enjoy running. After a couple of years of growth, I went back to a simpler business model by eliminating certain services and downsizing my staff.

It ended up being one of the best decisions I ever made as a business owner. I don't want to imply that I float into the office every day, blissfully enjoying every meeting, phone call and email. However, I do feel my work is much more aligned with my unique abilities, and to me this is what success is all about.

You may not be at a point in your career where you are able to pivot the way I did, but I have rarely found anyone who doesn't have the capacity to move closer to work they love and feel suited to do well. We will dig into how this works in the next chapter.

Build Meaningful Relationships

Aligning your work with your unique abilities is not enough. Just being in flow is not enough. I see clients every day who are doing the things they love and are suited for, but they are still stuck in the old paradigm of success – and still not achieving a sense of satisfaction.

I once had a client who couldn't wait to get to work every day – professionally, he was always in the zone. Additionally, he was regarded as one of the leaders in his industry, made a truckload of money, lived in a beautiful house and seemed to have it all. But, he didn't. No matter how much he enjoyed his career, his life was empty outside the office and that kept him from feeling the satisfaction that success promises.

What is the way out of this dilemma? The answer can be learned from the people who have the best perspective on how to define success: the people at the stage in life when they no longer care about how much money they're going to earn, what recognition they're going to get, or what acquisitions they piled up – that is, people at the end of their lives. At some point, we'll all have this clarity. Until then, we should pay attention to the insight of those who've gone before us and fold the lessons they learned into our own definition of success.

I studied four well-known books about the end of life:

- *Tuesdays with Morrie* by Mitch Albom – insights of an elderly man as told to a reporter from the *Detroit Free Press*.

- *The Last Lecture* by Randy Pausch – the final days of a computer science professor from Carnegie Mellon as he said goodbye to his students, wife and three children.

- *When Breath Becomes Air* by Paul Kalanithi – the story of a surgeon who fully understood what was taking place as his body was ravaged by cancer.

- *The Top Five Regrets of the Dying* by Bronnie Ware - insights from a hospice worker as she shares many different accounts from the patients she spent time with in their final days.

Despite their differences, these stories had a handful of similar themes. I began to see that two of these life lessons were so important that they absolutely needed to be a part of any definition of success.

First, the individuals facing the end all discussed the importance of their family and closest friends. As they reflected on their life, each talked about how they wished they could have more time with the people they loved the most. They regretted not telling them how much they valued their relationship and the impact they made on their life.

This should come as no surprise.

If I asked, *"What's most important in your life?"* you'd certainly list a person before anything else. You like your house, your car, your vacations and all the recognition your hard work delivers, but you love your kids, spouse, parents, siblings and closest friends. At the end, when you've got the best perspective you'll ever have, the difference between "like" and "love" is wider than the Grand Canyon.

Years ago, a dear friend and psychologist, Dr. Greg Sipes, told me, *"Life is only about relationships."* He didn't say that relationships were important or that we should spend more time with those we love. He used the world "only" for an important reason. He's learned after seeing thousands of patients over the last thirty years that when you come right down to it, nothing else matters. Not your job, your house, personal net worth or even your kid's batting average in youth baseball – nothing, nada, zilch.

You've seen this at work in your own life if you ever lost someone you loved dearly before their time. The pain you felt was crushing and much worse than losing a job or even declaring bankruptcy. On more than one occasion in my life I've thought, as long as I've got my family, I can handle anything. I've never said that about my business, house, retirement account or anything else that I might be tempted to brag about on Facebook.

Once I was reminded that life is *only* about relationships, I realized any definition of success would be incomplete without including this idea.

Enjoy the Journey

Next, my research into these end-of-life stories highlighted an additional concept that I hadn't considered. Each of the individuals discussed a simple idea that seemed so obvious, I didn't see it at first. As soon as it hit me, I realized that it may just be the most important piece of the happiness puzzle. These courageous people helped me to understand that we need to do a better job of enjoying the journey.

Bronnie Ware found that the people she cared for wish that they had *"let themselves be happier."* Randy Pausch reminded us to "never underestimate the importance of having fun," and perfectly drove this point home during his *Last Lecture:* "I'm dying and I'm having fun. And I'm going to keep having fun every day because there's no other way to play it….Having fun for me is like a fish talking about the importance of water."

This revelation hit extremely close to home.

Throughout the majority of my professional life, I have wondered on multiple occasions if I am really "enjoying the journey." Researching for this book brought this question front and center. It helped me to see that until about few years ago, I rarely took the time to slow down and "smell the flowers along the way." I was always rushing on to the next big achievement. Slowing down and enjoying the scenery was for other people who didn't have the same aspirations, talent and skill as the amazing CJ.

I distinctly recall one particular incident about ten years ago.

For the previous eighteen months, I had been obsessed with landing a spot on the *Indianapolis Business Journal's* "40 under 40," a list of the top up-and-coming business leaders in the marketplace. I was convinced that as soon as I was recognized as one of the best, I could sit back and really enjoy my success. That list represented an important milestone in my career and I strived to meet it. Eventually, in 2006, I made the list. I was featured in a supplement to the paper and received a whole bunch of recognition from friends, family and business associates. It was great – for about a week. I soon felt driven to move on to the next big objective. I'm sure I was thinking, "The other members of this '40 under 40' class are probably on to their next achievement, I can't fall behind."

Do I sound like someone you may know?

Don't feel guilty, you're not alone. It turns out that 97.5% (made-up statistic) of the professionals I've met over the years don't regularly take the time to slow down and appreciate their accomplishments. They're just like you and me – checking the achievement/recognition box and then moving on to bigger and better goals, saying to themselves, "I can't spend all day relishing my environment or I'll fall behind all my fellow overachievers."

There are two responses to this argument.

First, there's zero evidence to indicate that enjoying the journey will result in you getting trampled while the other overachievers crawl over your loafing body to reach the next professional plateau. You can do both. You can have both!

Second, who really gives a shit if you do fall a little behind? Actually answer that. Who would notice? Who would care? I bet the list is very short. And are the people on it people you actually admire? Probably not.

I challenge you and every other overachieving professional on the planet to consider the following question: "Was I put on this earth to enjoy its beauty, the people on it and the experiences it provides, or am I here to simply earn more money, recognition and stuff than everybody else?" Your answer to this question will determine the amount of satisfaction and happiness you enjoy for the rest of your life. It's highly probable at this point you're thinking, "I'll promise to start really focusing on enjoying the journey as soon as I..."

Unfortunately, this approach never works, because there will always be another "as soon as." It's time for you fully embrace the idea that the connection between achievement/recognition and happiness is tenuous at best. Realize that a big achievement may help you enjoy the journey for a short period of time, but you will almost always revert back to feeling that your current accomplishments are inadequate.

Trust me, I've worked with hundreds of overachieving professionals and I can promise you that the striving never stops, no matter how big the accomplishments. In fact, some of the most successful people are the ones who tend to become the most obsessed with the next big "win." They lose the ability to enjoy their accomplishments for even a moment. If you want to be satisfied, you need to slow down, step back and enjoy the roses every once in a while.

If you don't take any time to enjoy the journey, what's the real purpose of all your efforts?

No Definition is Perfect

As we discussed earlier, hundreds of brilliant scholars have a view on the definition of success and I think there's something valuable in each one. However, we both know how everything in your world is pushing you to think about the concept in terms of money, stuff, and recognition, etc.

It's time to shift your paradigm and think differently about success. Once again, here's the definition I recommend you consider going forward:

Success is… The extent to which I utilize my unique abilities, build meaningful relationships and enjoy the journey.

At first glance, these short sixteen words may almost seem too simple to make a big difference in your life. How can they inspire a paradigm shift? They can – I have seen it happen in my practice time after time. Living by these three guidelines will completely change your perspective.

- You'll think differently about the amount of hours you spend at work.

- You'll spend less time comparing your achievements with others.

- You'll find more opportunities to schedule time with your family and close friends.

- You'll feel less stress as you decrease the amount of energy you put towards obsessing about your next achievement.

- You'll begin to see the beauty in everyday circumstances.

- You'll become more empathetic and do a better job of listening to others.

- You'll do a better job of prioritizing things that really matter in your life.

- Your spiritual life will improve.

- You'll likely feel healthier, sleep better and may even lose some weight.

- You'll enjoy more happiness and satisfaction.

- And odds are good that your achievements will continue to pile up at the same rate they did before. It's a win-win-win.

Now, it looks like you've really got yourself quite a dilemma. Should I keep on my current path, earn a bunch of money, get lots of stuff and make sure my peers understand what a successful person I've become? Or, do I try to follow a different approach and trust that it delivers all of the benefits CJ's promising (and that all seem to make really good sense)?

It's a tricky quandary, but something tells me that if you've made it this far you're ready to try something different.

As you can see, the benefits are significant and there's virtually no downside. But, just like anything that's really important in life, realizing these benefits requires change and that change is extremely difficult for most overachieving professionals. You're up against your entire history, almost everyone you know, and a colossal advertising and marketing apparatus that utilizes a simple message to entice you to believe you need their products and services. The marketing machine bombards with messages that say you lack something in your life (hair, a house with a pool, rock hard abs, a Caribbean vacation). They employ this strategy for one reason – it works. The challenge becomes more difficult when you sprinkle in social media, which encourages the world to share every achievement and acquisition in real time with everyone you know.

The deck is stacked against you.

But, despite these odds, I know you can change, and I'm committed to helping you get there. The rest of this book will provide you with powerful strategies to begin living by this new definition of success. I'm not going to promise you an overnight transformation. But I will guarantee that by the time you read the final page, you'll be inspired to change, feel a significant amount of momentum to do so, and have a collection of simple tactics to keep you moving in the right direction.

Let's get to work.

Three Key Points to Remember

1. The perspective through which you view the world is heavily influenced by certain paradigms. These concepts were developed over years and are extremely hard to change. For example, if you grew up in Ann Arbor and attended Michigan you probably believe that all evil in the world originates in Columbus, OH.

2. As an overachiever, you've followed a paradigm since elementary school that implies that the only way to feel success is to "work extremely hard so that you earn tons of recognition/money/acquisitions." This paradigm influences every single decision that you make and has delivered everything it's promised – except the satisfaction and happiness you really hope to achieve.

3. The first step in your journey towards contentment is exploring your definition of success. There are limitless ways to look at this concept, including hard work, perseverance, doing your best, making a difference, etc. I think all of these are valuable. However, after spending years exploring the question and applying different models to my clients, I've developed the following description. I believe success is: *"The extent to which I utilize my unique abilities, build meaningful relationships and enjoy the journey."*

Chapter 2 – Taking Action

In this chapter, you learned that your current definition of success affects every decision that you make. In this exercise, I'm going to challenge you to explore how this paradigm has negatively impacted your happiness over the years. Here's how this works.

1. Select at least three examples of decisions you've made in your life that were influenced by your need to chase after success.

2. Talk about the beliefs that led you to make these decisions.

3. Detail the negative consequences of these decisions.

You can complete this exercise in the space below or by downloading a template at CoachCJ.com/bookexercises.

Decision	Why?	Consequences
Started my first job one week after graduating from college instead of going on a long trip to Europe with my friends.	I wanted to ensure that I got the job and was also interested in getting ahead of every other recent graduate.	I missed a once-in-a-lifetime opportunity to explore different cultures to start a job that I quit after less than 2 years.

	Decision	Why?	Consequences
1			
2			
3			
4			
5			

Be Yourself

"Why fit in when you were born to stand out!"
                                        – Dr. Seuss

I have a good friend, Peter Dunn, who is unusual for a bunch of different reasons. One of those is that he actually really enjoys his job. He can't wait to get to work each day and does what he truly loves from the moment he walks in the office until he closes his laptop at the day's end.

Pete came from a family of entrepreneurs and this influence led him to major in business administration in college. After being inspired by a fun class in the fifth grade where he was able to trade stocks, Pete decided he wanted to get into the financial industry. Upon graduation, he took a job at Met Life and after a few successful years selling life insurance, he moved on to a career in financial planning, where he had a lot of success and built a healthy book of business.

Another quality that makes Pete a little unusual is that he was a standup comedian in college. He loved making people laugh and soon realized that he got a ton of energy and enjoyment from entertaining. Becoming a standup comedian didn't seem like a "real job," so he decided to follow the more logical and safe route into the financial industry. The ability to make a live audience laugh seemed like an impossible skill to integrate into his worklife.

After a few years running his own financial planning business, Pete ran into an opportunity to work with a couple who had a combined annual income of more than $400,000 (which in central Indiana is a lot of money). He tells a great story about the night he sat in their driveway eagerly anticipating the opportunity to land a new client who appeared to have a solid financial foundation. A little more than an hour later, Pete left discouraged and amazed that a couple who made that much money could barely figure out a way to pay all their bills, much less put anything into savings.

Over the years, he began to run into these types of situations more and more often and found himself spending a significant amount of his time helping these people manage their expenses and build budgets instead of focusing on investment recommendations.

This experience inspired Pete to start writing a blog called *"Things Your Dad Never Taught You About Money."* He found out fast that he loved writing about these issues in his very unique, entertaining style. More importantly, he got a great deal of satisfaction answering laypeople's questions about their money issues. He felt that for the first time he was making a meaningful difference in the lives of people who needed it the most.

After a few years writing blogs and publishing his first book, a large financial services company contacted Pete and asked if he could train their staff about how to more effectively manage their money. Pete built a compelling curriculum, taught live sessions and was instantly hooked. He had a rare gift for explaining a complex subject in a way that made it simple to understand. More importantly, his approach made the audience feel like he was on the journey with them. In between the laughter and sometimes the tears, Pete had discovered a way to connect with a group of people that were completely frustrated with their financial situations. He gave them hope and a plan they could believe in – and he was utilizing his unique talents. It was a win-win situation.

One engagement led to another and after a few more years, Pete decided to sell his financial planning business and dedicate himself fulltime to the brand of "Pete the Planner," a financial coach/trainer/author who uses humor and straightforward, simple advice that doesn't just teach people, but actually inspires them to change.

Today, he's a nationally recognized expert on helping individuals get control of their finances. He's been featured on *Good Morning America* and writes a weekly column for *USA Today*. The more he follows his passion and utilizes his unique abilities, the happier he gets, and guess what? His business continues to grow.

Why We Ignore Our Unique Abilities

Unlike Pete, most individuals spend the majority of their professional lives doing something that has very little to do with their unique abilities, skills or interest. Chances are good that this includes you.

Don't beat yourself up too much; it's not all your fault. From a very early age, most children are funneled by a well-intentioned school system into a very narrow path that's designed to ensure that everyone learns the same skills before they move on to college or the "real world."

This process has been cemented in society for several millennia. Before anyone legislated that young people had to attend school, early thinkers had opinions about its purpose. In the fourth century BC, the famous Greek philosopher Plato felt that education existed to "ensure that the habit and aspirations of the old generation are transmitted to the younger – and then presumably to the next one after that."[iv] Approximately one hundred years later, Aristotle offered the following opinion: "Education is a function of the State, and is conducted, primarily at least, for the ends of the State."[v] In other words, two of the world's most influential thinkers both believed that school existed simply to make sure information was passed on to serve the greater needs of society as a whole.

Fast forward two thousand years. In 1988, noted educational historian David Tyack argued that the purpose of school has always been to further social and economic needs.[vi] Less than a decade after this statement, prominent sociologists K.B Demaris and M.D. LeCompte wrote that school had a pragmatic purpose with four major purposes that include:

- Intellectual purposes such as the development of mathematical and reading skills;

---

iv   G.K. Plochmann, *Plato* (New York: Dell Pub. Co., 1973), 74-75.
v   Elizabeth Mays, "Aristotle on Education," last modified April 30, 2014, http://www.newfoundations.com/GALLERY/Aristotle.html.
vi   David Tyack, "Ways of seeing: An essay on the history of compulsory schooling," *Harvard Educational Review* 46, no. 3 (1976).

- Political purposes such as the assimilation of immigrants;

- Economic purposes such as job preparation; and

- Social purposes such as the development of social and moral responsibility.

Can you see that a general theme has been reinforced over time? Educational systems have been designed to prepare students in a very similar fashion to accomplish very similar goals once they depart for the next phase of their lives.

The idea that the system is built to produce a legion of young adults with similar skills and interests is cemented even further when you consider the concept of standardized testing. The idea that we should develop a method for measuring baseline intelligence first took root in the early 1800s and by 1918 more than one hundred different tests had been developed to understand the proficiency of students in primary and secondary education.[vii] By 1935, high speed computing allowed electronic data processing to "process massive numbers of tests."[viii] Since then, the testing industry has exploded, and we as a nation have become obsessed with ensuring that all of our students have the same fundamental intellectual capabilities in a handful of subjects such as math, reading, and science.

Today, largely due to the *No Child Left Behind* Act of 2001, all students are tested from third grade through eighth to ensure

---

vii   Dan Fletcher, "Standardized Testing," Time, December 11, 2009, http://content.time.com/time/nation/article/0,8599,1947019,00.htm.

viii   Paulina Alcocer, "History of Standardized Testing in the United States," NEA, accessed March 15, 2017, http://www.nea.org/home/66139.htm.

that they reach "proficiency" in reading and math[ix] (In 2012, President Obama granted many states waivers to this law – but nearly all of these states still have a form of standardized test in these grades). In addition, nearly all states have a standardized test in high school to measure similar types of proficiencies.[x] Finally, as you well know, in order to get admitted to college you need to do well on either the SAT or ACT.

In short, we've created an educational machine throughout the United States that teaches our children the exact same curriculum and then tests them annually (at the minimum) to ensure that they're grasping the same fundamental concepts. All of this is done in the hope that once they leave school they are ready to be productive members of society – and as similar to one another as possible.

Now, before I say one more word and risk infuriating every teacher on the planet, I want to make a few things abundantly clear:

- This summary is not intended to be critical of the school system in America or the concept of standardized testing. I am not an expert in education and don't understand the issues well enough to have a dog in this fight. I am simply stating the facts.

- Teachers are probably the most undervalued professionals in our country. For the past nine years, I have sent my kids to a public school where selfless individuals have spent more

---

ix   "No Child Left Behind Act," Wikipedia, last modified March 11, 2017, https://en.wikipedia.org/wiki/No_Child_Left_Behind_Act#Replacement.

x   "List of state achievement tests in the United States," Wikipedia, last modified March 03, 2017, https://en.wikipedia.org/wiki/List_of_state_achievement_tests_in_the_United_States

time each day mentoring and teaching them than I do and they have *never* had anything but outstanding teachers. I couldn't be more grateful for their efforts.

- The high school guidance counselors that I've met (who are supposed to help students identify what they really enjoy) are typically assigned hundreds of kids and asked do to the impossible job of giving each one individual attention.

That being said, despite the best intentions, our school systems aren't designed, and aren't even capable in many instances, of encouraging young people to explore their unique abilities and interests – unless, of course, you love excelling in a handful of subjects and taking standardized tests.

This scenario is more pronounced for overachievers because we crave being measured and recognized for our achievements – even if it means completely ignoring what we enjoy doing the most. Outdoing our peers by getting the best grades and admission to the top college is ALL that matters.

Accordingly, most overachieving students enter college assuming the game is still the same. Even though there are certainly more opportunities to explore many different interests in college, we typically follow a similar formula – work your ass off to get the best grades so that you can land the highest paying, most prestigious job, regardless of what the job entails. Time spent in extracurricular activities has only one purpose: improve the resume. If you happen to uncover a fun interest along the way, that's a lucky bonus – but the truth is that most people don't follow impractical passions like sociology or ceramics.

The hard-working overachiever is often rewarded with multiple job opportunities. Several years later, they've advanced in their careers and built a great lifestyle around a growing income. Then, one day they wake up and realize that this is the profession they'll have for the rest of their lives; there appears to be no way out. They can't go back and become a doctor or a lawyer or switch gears to start over again and become an actor or a chef. They may not be *miserable* – they're just stuck doing something that 94.6% (another made up statistic) of the time isn't utilizing their unique talents, skills or interests, and it begins to grate on them.

As I said before, being stuck is not your fault. You mastered the rules of a well-intentioned system and are now a very productive (and well-compensated) member of society. Congratulations.

Don't be discouraged. You're not just an overachieving robot who's been programmed to chase money, recognition and stuff with no hope of ever finding any satisfaction in your life. You're an unbelievably gifted hard worker who's simply questioning the current approach. This is an extremely healthy process that's an important part of your journey.

Do as I Say, Not as I Do

How can you get into the state of flow in your own life where you get more enjoyment and satisfaction from all your hard work? That depends on a variety of factors that we'll explore in depth later in this chapter.

Before we do, let me tell you about an overachiever who bounced all over the place before he figured out what he really enjoyed and finally pursued his passion. That guy is me, and you can learn by *not* doing what I did.

I was a political science major, and like many political science and history majors, I applied to law school. Once I was accepted, I assumed it was karma telling me that I was destined to become an attorney.

It turns out that I wasn't destined for that profession in any way. After less than a semester in law school, I realized that the last thing I wanted to do was to become a lawyer and quit. So, there I was in the winter of 1994, a law school dropout with a political science degree. A truly magical combination.

Instead of taking an inventory of my interests, skills and abilities, I opened up the yellow pages, went to "political organizations" and scrolled down to find the Republican State Central Committee. I called them up, and as luck would have it, they needed an Assistant Operations Director (aka glorified intern).

I took the job, eventually became the Operations Director and for three years learned a bunch about how to run a small team and the ins and outs of campaign finance (a skill that's completely useless outside of politics, in case you were wondering). In 1996, after recognizing that just about all politicians are full of shit, I decided it was time to try something new. If you think this is the point in the story where I quietly reflected on what I really wanted to do in life, think again.

Instead, I reached out to a good friend of mine who was working at one of the Big 5 accounting firms – Arthur Andersen – and asked if he thought there was any way I could get a job with their business consulting group. Somehow, I convinced his boss that my background was perfect for their team, and I started out as a business analyst.

Less than two years later, my former boss in politics, who also owned a private equity firm, called me up and asked if I had any interest in helping to run a small company that made soap and shampoo for hotels. Assuming the grass was always going to be greener, I thought, "Why not?" and made the shift.

For the first time in my professional career I stumbled upon something that truly interested me – small business. I was fascinated with all aspects of the company, worked a ton of hours, made truckloads of mistakes, and thought maybe I'd found my calling.

In the spring of 2000, I decided to ignore this "calling" when some of my old Arthur Andersen buddies contacted me to come and work for a "dot-com" company that was about to explode. They offered a pay raise and something called "stock options" that were certain to make me a multi-millionaire, and so, lured by the promise of big, easy money, I jumped again.

If you remember anything about the Internet "bubble" you can probably guess that I didn't get rich. After three-plus years bouncing all over the company (marketing, sales, project management, IT) and complaining about how incompetent the leadership team was, I decided it was time to really figure out what I wanted to do when I grew up.

I started meeting with a bunch of different professionals and asking them about their careers. For the first time in my life, I was focused on taking an inventory of my interests. One of the possibilities I considered was starting my own business. It would allow me to combine my wide background and fulfill my desire to be the "boss." This path led me to a Franchise "broker" who put me through a handful of tests and helped me understand what type of company would be a good fit for my interests, abilities and background.

A few months later, I had drained our savings account, quit my job (five days before we had our first child. I know, brilliant move) and started a business coaching enterprise in my basement. Despite the fact that Year #1 was terrifying, this turned out to be the best professional move of my life.

It forced me way outside my comfort zone, which it turned out I enjoyed. More importantly, the move allowed me the freedom to test a variety of different approaches to see what I liked the best. I started out by coaching small business owners. Next, I decided to add a class for entrepreneurs, which resulted in a packed schedule, employees, and a growing top line. When I quickly realized that I wasn't blessed with the patience to coach entrepreneurs in a classroom setting, I shut down the program, reduced staff and went back to the drawing board to figure out the BEST fit for my unique abilities. It didn't take long for me to return to coaching overachieving professionals, and my love of teaching led me to write this book.

As you can clearly see, finding what I love didn't happen overnight, it wasn't easy and it required me to zig-zag all over the place, but I found work that I know is absolutely perfect for me. It took me three years, but I did it – and if I can do it, so can you.

What Makes You Unique?

As you can see from my story, figuring out how to best utilize your unique abilities can be challenging, but *identifying* what makes you different from everyone else is easier than you think, and is a powerful exercise no matter where you are in your career trajectory. I often ask my private coaching clients to do this, and many are C-level execs at multi-million dollar companies. They often balk at first – "CJ, come on, isn't that a little basic?" – but it ends up being the foundation of the satisfaction that escapes them.

There are a handful of proven tactics that can help you figure out your unique skills. The process will require you to first make a subtle shift in your mindset. Instead of acting like an accomplished overachiever who's got everything figured out, you'll need to begin thinking like a five-year-old on his or her first day of pre-school. By that I mean, consider becoming *wildly curious* about everything in your environment. That includes everything you read, listen to or watch, and every person you encounter in your personal and professional life. This slight shift will help make the process far more efficient and effective.

The method I'm going to lay out has many different steps. I would recommend that you complete each one to gain the most insight into what makes you tick. As you get into the work, you may find that some of the steps are far more valuable to you than others. Be patient, this is part of the plan. From one overachiever to another, I promise none of this activity is a waste of time.

Your Five Top Skills

Identifying what makes you different/unique is a little bit like painting a picture. This process will highlight lots of different colors (concepts/ideas/themes/patterns) that at times work nicely together and seem to create a clear image. But don't be alarmed if the colors clash and you feel the need to scrap the whole thing and start from scratch – it's part of the process.

A great way to start is by taking an inventory of your current abilities/interests to identify five skills that best reflect what makes you unique. The following exercise will help you select your top five. Here's how it works:

1. Download and print off the list[xi] of skills/abilities at CoachCJ.com/bookexercises and get a high-level sense of the types of abilities it includes.

2. Cross out any ability that clearly represents an exact *opposite* of the skills you possess. These are items you hate doing or for which you have absolutely zero aptitude. When I first completed this exercise, I crossed out a ton, including "Attention to Detail" and "Patience."

3. Cross out those abilities that you've got, but that you don't enjoy all that much and certainly don't want to be part of your everyday life. For me, that included "Technical Work" and "Dealing with Complaints." Now that the list has probably been cut by at least 50–60%, we'll start to focus on what is the best fit for you.

4. Put a checkmark next to every phrase that you feel represents something that you would enjoy. Transfer these to the chart on page 58. You should limit this list to no more than fifteen.

5. Look at these fifteen entries and select the five that you believe are best represented by the following four statements:

    ○ I get excited when I even think about doing this.

    ○ I could do this all day long five days a week.

    ○ This comes naturally and easily for me.

xi   "Examples of Skills," YourDictionary, accessed March 15, 2017, http://examples.yourdictionary.com/examples-of-skills.html.

º My past behavior has clearly demonstrated that I have
this ability.

Now, you've got a list of five abilities that are a solid repre-
sentation of your current skills and interests. I would write these
down on a Post-It Note® and put it someplace you look at all
the time. These five words/phrases will provide you with a great
foundation upon which you begin figuring out what you'd love
to spend the rest of your life doing.

I will concede (for the highly analytical overachiever) that
this isn't exactly scientific. Understanding the fact that this is
simply an exercise you breezed through while reading a book, it's
entirely possible that you missed something. That's okay – don't
panic. We're not getting these words tattooed on your forearm
– you can always add/subtract as you learn more.

Top 15

Skill/Ability

1	
2	
3	
4	
5	
6	
7	

Skill/Ability

8	
9	
10	
11	
12	
13	
14	
15	

Top 5

Skill/Ability

1	
2	
3	
4	
5	

Professional Assessments

Next, I recommend that you turn to the experts and find out if their analysis supports what you learned in the above exercise. The "experts" I am referring to are organizations that have spent years writing books and developing assessments that are designed to help you figure out what makes you different from everyone else.

As you can imagine, there are a ton of assessment resources available and each one takes a slightly different approach. You'll find some to be extremely valuable and others to be a waste of time. Regardless, this research is an important part of the process. I recommend that you select three outside resources to supplement the work you've already completed. Less than that can give you a narrow view of the landscape and more just gets overwhelming.

I've taken tons of assessments in my coaching work and I don't think it matters all that much which one you use. Each one provides a slightly different viewpoint, many of which can be useful. Here's some high-level guidance to help you select a few options. I've grouped these resources into three categories and offered an overview, including a few examples from the marketplace.

Personal/Career Interest Assessment – These assessments will help you identify the types of activities you like and don't like. The tools are extremely helpful in helping you figure out which types of careers are the best fit for your unique abilities. The best recognized are the *Strong Interest Inventory* and the *MAPP™ Career Assessment Test,* but there are a ton of others to choose from.

Personality/Behavioral Assessment – You are probably most familiar with the tests in this group. These types of assessments are focused on empirically measuring a handful of personality "traits and styles" to help you understand how you interpret information in your environment. This will affect the way you communicate with others and make decisions on a daily basis. These are the ones I've seen used the most:

- *DISC Profile* – This is my favorite for a handful of reasons: it's inexpensive (less than $40 per test), it only takes about ten minutes to complete, it's extremely easy to understand the results and it's unbelievably accurate.

- *Myers-Briggs* – Introspective self-reporting questionnaire that's designed to tell an individual how they perceive the world.

- *Predictive Index* – Skill and behavior assessment test used to help determine how employees will deal with work situations or different types of managers.

- *Core Values Index* – Assessment that provides a description of the "innate, unchanging nature of an individual, which is different from personality and behavioral based assessments."[xii]

Skills/Abilities Assessment – This category of tests aims to measure an individual's ability to reason, understand and solve problems. These can be very general (e.g. SAT) in nature or designed specifically for a unique skill (e.g. Microsoft Excel Aptitude Test). You'll have to take this type of test in one form or another

xii   "Taylor Protocols - The Core Values Index," Taylor Protocols, accessed March 13, 2017, https://www.taylorprotocols.com/CVI.php.

at some point in your life for educational or professional purposes. The number to choose from is unlimited, which makes it nearly impossible to recommend any one assessment.

Typically, most people don't feel the need to take this type of a test in the middle of their career. However, if you are interested in learning more about this specific category, I would suggest you Google "Cognitive Assessment Test" and find one that you feel will provide you with the best insight into your skills/abilities. I recently took the *Wonderlic® Personnel Test – Quicktest* and thought the results provided valuable insight.

Building a Core Team of Advisors

Once you have a solid understanding of your skills and aptitudes, I suggest that you enlist the help of others for the rest of this journey. These trusted individuals will provide an outside perspective and support for the times when you run into the inevitable challenges that come with introspection. In addition, they can offer valuable insight into a professional path you may have never considered.

First, build a core team of advisors/friends/mentors with the following characteristics:

- You are married to this person. Your spouse absolutely must be involved.

- You have a close relationship and long history.

- They're committed to helping you discover your unique abilities.

- They're not afraid to provide you with honest feedback. You may have worked for them in the past.

You don't need to schedule a formal meeting with an agenda, white board and "next steps" on a regular interval with this group. Rather, I'd suggest that you meet with each of them individually on a regular basis to discuss your progress and ask for their input.

Initially, here's the kind of insight I suggest you get from this team of supporters. Ask them for their candid feedback on the following questions:

- What do you think I enjoy doing the most – personally and professionally?

- What do think are my unique skills, abilities and interests?

- What do I seem to hate doing? In other words, what do I bitch and complain about the most?

- How do you think I can expand or change my work life to better utilize my unique skills?

- Can you think of any hobbies or side gigs that would utilize my unique skills?

- If there were no limitations whatsoever, what do you think would be the ideal career for me?

By the end of these conversations you should have uncovered a handful of themes or patterns that will add color to the picture you're painting. Don't be surprised if you get conflicting opinions – not everyone is exposed to you in exactly the same environment. Also, don't worry if the feedback seems to contradict the five skills/abilities you identified in the first exercise. Remember, you're painting a picture and the more colors the better – even if they don't seem to go together at first.

If you are looking for a career change, one of the great outcomes of these conversations will be when your advisors begin to suggest different careers that you might want to consider. This advice will often be accompanied by an offer to introduce you to someone in this field who could provide you with additional insight.

What Do I Do With All This Information?

At this point, you've completed a handful of valuable exercises:

- Completed a Personal Inventory designed to identify your top five skills/interests.

- Taken a handful of "Professional" assessments focused on your career, personality and skills/interests.

- Discussed your personal profile with the people in your life who know you the best.

- Interviewed professionals to learn more about their unique careers.

Now that you've gathered all of this data, it's time to see if any patterns emerge that point you toward a set of interests or abilities that really get you excited. Hopefully, the painting is really starting to take shape, but if it isn't, don't be alarmed. All that means is that you've got some more research to do. I promise that diligently following this process will eventually lead you to an "a-ha" moment, where you at the very least find yourself leaning in a certain direction.

Once you land on a handful of interests and abilities that you feel are best for you, and you get support from your team of trusted advisors, it's time to take some action. Before you make any rash decisions, I encourage you to ask a few important questions:

1. *Does my current professional path allow me to effectively make use of my unique skills and talents on a **regular** basis?* If your answer is "yes," then consider yourself very lucky and enjoy the ride. If your answer is "no," then you need to move on to the next question.

2. *Is there a reasonably good opportunity that I could figure out a way (e.g. change, divisions, responsibilities, jobs within the industry, etc.) to develop these skills and abilities?* If the answer is "yes," then I would pursue that option. For example, if you work for a huge publically traded company, there's many different places where you can flex your unique muscles. If your answer is "no," you need to move on to the next question.

3. *Am I in a healthy position to do a complete 180 and try something brand new?* Here's what I mean by "healthy position": if you have four kids, three of whom are in college and the change you're considering making would instantly cut your income by 50%, then I wouldn't recommend you tender your resignation anytime soon. In other words, if your answer is "no," you are not in a healthy positon to make a radical change. That doesn't mean, however, that you just simply give up on figuring out a way to participate in the activities you love. Rather, I urge you to consider looking outside your work

for opportunities to engage your interests and abilities. For example, if you find that you've got a passion for teaching, volunteer at a local after school tutoring program or a weekend adult education course.

On the flip side, if you are in a "healthy" financial position (no dependent kids, money in savings, spouse who works, low monthly expenses, etc.) then I would suggest that you consider a serious change and do something completely different.

Now that you understand the significance of getting clarity around what makes you unique, it's time to explore the second part of the formula: building meaningful relationships. In the next chapter I'll explain why getting the most satisfaction out of your life is almost impossible without significant personal and professional friendships.

<u>Three Key Points to Remember</u>

1. Many overachievers neglect to identify their unique abilities because our society pushes these "Type A" individuals into careers that offer the greatest recognition and pay. It's extremely difficult to get off of this success "train" that most of us board in fifth or sixth grade.

2. Identifying your unique skills/abilities/interests is a critical component to getting more satisfaction out of your life. This process isn't easy and doesn't happen overnight. I recommend a handful of simple strategies that will help get you going:

   ° Identify your top five skills/abilities

   ° Take a handful of personal and professional assessments

   ° Build a team of advisors

3. Once you've developed a little clarity around what makes you distinct, it's time for action. The next step in your journey depends on a variety of factors:

   ° Does your current profession allow you to utilize your unique skills? If yes, congrats!

   ° Could you move within your company to utilize your abilities more effectively?

   ° If the answer to the above question is "no," are you in a position to pivot and start something completely different?

   ° If you can't leave your current career and start over, what are the extracurricular opportunities that allow you to engage these skills?

Chapter 3 – Taking Action

In his groundbreaking research Mihaly Csikszentmihalyi (impossible to pronounce, don't even try it) introduced the concept of "flow," which he described as "a state of concentration or complete absorption with the activity at hand and the situation. It is a state in which people are so involved in an activity that nothing else seems to matter."[xiii]

In this exercise, you're going to identify areas of your life when you felt like you were in a state of flow and how you could introduce this type of experience into your everyday life.

1. Select at least one example of a time when you felt completely absorbed in an activity you enjoyed so much that nothing else seemed to matter.

2. Decide on an activity that you could participate in which would help you get back into this state of mind. Note: this may not come to you immediately – that's OK. Now that you're clear about the experience, you'll eventually identify an activity.

You can complete this exercise in the space below or by downloading a template at CoachCJ.com/bookexercises.

---

xiii   Mihaly Csikszentmihalyi, *Flow: the Psychology of Optimal Experience* (New York: Harper Perennial Modern Classics, 2008).

Experience	Current Activity
I absolutely love singing and performing. I remember being in a state of "flow" when I was the lead singer for a local band in college.	I could volunteer to sing in the church band.

	Experience	Current Activity
1		
2		
3		

CHAPTER 4

Build Together

"Relationships are more important than life, but it is important for those relationships to have life in them."
— Swami Vivikananda

On a bright sunny morning in the fall of 2001, America was forever changed when a plane hijacked by terrorists slammed into the north tower of the World Trade Center at approximately 8:45am.

Depending on your age, you remember exactly where you were the morning of September 11, 2001. Chances are that you also remember how you felt and what you did as soon as you learned about the attack.

I was working at a small software company in Indianapolis when I first saw the images of a huge hole in the side of the north tower on CNN.com. Seconds later, I called my wife to make sure she knew what was going on in New York. I then packed up my laptop, jumped in my car and drove to my parents who lived about five minutes from my office.

We sat in silence watching the events unfold.

As soon as the south tower collapsed just before 10:00 a.m., I picked up the phone and called my two closest friends from college. I was able to reach Tom, who lived in Chicago, but due to jammed phone lines, was unable to get in touch with Dan, who lived in New York City. We later learned he was okay.

That night, my wife and I had dinner with my closest friend Kevin and his wife Kim. We sat quietly at an O'Charley's, picked over our food, thought about all the people who had suffered so much loss, and reflected on one of the darkest days in US history. For one of the first times in my life, I had very little to say.

I bet your experience that day was similar to mine. You were stunned by the news and shocked to your core. Nothing like this had ever happened in your lifetime, and you immediately wanted to lean on something familiar and important. So, you connected with the people who meant the most to you.

When we are faced with an important event in our lives, whether traumatic (9/11) or joyous (just got engaged), we need to share that experience with the people we love the most because those relationships are all that really matter. This core value is one of the few characteristics that nearly all humans share – including those who were lost on September 11, 2001.

At 9:47 a.m., Ceecee Lyles, a flight attendant on Flight 93 that ultimately crashed in Stoney Creek, Pennsylvania, called her husband as she frantically watched a crew put together a plan to rush the cabin and overtake the terrorists. Her voicemail said, "Please tell my children that I love them very much. I'm sorry, baby. I wish I could see your face again."

Thirty-one year old Melissa Harrington was in a meeting in the north tower the morning of September 11th. First, she called her father Bob, and then her husband Sean who was asleep. "Sean, it's me," she said in her message. "I just wanted to let you know I love you and I'm stuck in this building in New York. There's a lot of smoke and I just wanted to let you know that I love you always."[xiv]

Captain Walter Hynes of the New York Fire Department's Ladder 13 called his wife on his way to Lower Manhattan, where he helped people in the north tower find their way down the stairs towards safety. His message was simple: "I don't know if we'll make it out. I want to tell you that I love you and I love the kids."[xv]

Nearly three thousand people were killed on the morning of September 11, 2001, and I'm certain that once they knew something terrible was happening, every single person who was able to do so immediately reached out to someone they loved. No one made sure to finish up an email or call a big client. When push comes to shove, relationships are *all* that matters. Everything else is irrelevant.

The Difference Between Knowing and Doing

We all know how valuable relationships are in our lives. If someone asks you what is most important, you will undoubtedly rattle off the names of your closest family members and friends. I've asked this question of thousands of people in my life and never has someone mentioned their job, car or country club membership. Not one time.

Despite the unanimous agreement that nothing else matters

---

xiv   Maria Hinojosa, "On September 11, final words of love," CNN, September 10, 2002, http://edition.cnn.com/2002/US/09/03/ar911.phone.calls/.
xv   Peggy Noonan, "The Sounds That Still Echo From 9/11," *The Wall Street Journal*, September 9, 2006, https://www.wsj.com/articles/SB115774704992357920.

as much as the people we love, I rarely find behavior supporting this belief in overachievers. Instead, I witness professionals working long hours, taking their laptops on vacations, and staying glued to their phones during every extracurricular "family" event, such as sports or musical performances.

We claim that family is most important, but our behavior tells a completely different story. Here's a quick exercise to help you understand the value you place on the most significant relationships in life.

1. Take out your calendar and review a typical week (Monday – Sunday) in your life.

2. Assume the following behaviors take up approximately eighty hours, or 50% of your week:

   ○ Sleep = fifty hours a week

   ○ Eating = twenty hours a week

   ○ Bathing = ten hours per week

3. Now, without overthinking it too much, document where you spend the remaining eighty-eight hours.

My guess is that you came up with a number that indicates around fifty hours per week on work, twenty hours on other things like exercise and entertainment, and somewhere in the neighborhood of eighteen hours on the people you love. That's the typical breakdown I see in the clients I work with. Are you surprised that what you claim to be the most important thing in your life gets such a small percentage of your time? Overachievers often are – and then they become embarrassed or frustrated or angry at the reality, because it's not a reality that aligns with their belief system. This simple exercise indicates that your relationships may only be important in theory. Or, as Stephen Covey puts it, "To know and not to do is really not to know."

I assume this isn't the first time you've thought to yourself, *"I should be spending more time with my kids, spouse, close friends, and family."* In your gut, you've always known that there's a discrepancy between what you say is important and how you prioritize daily activities. Those kinds of discrepancies can cause stress in our lives and our relationships, and even in our souls. Not living according to our beliefs can eat away at us. Which begs the question: what's the problem? Why don't we just rearrange our schedules and get things back in balance?

The answer is fairly simple and straightforward. As I mentioned in the first chapter, we've been hardwired from an early age to focus our behavior towards activities that earn external recognition. Working a ton of hours leads to more money, a better job title, and a bigger house. There's no place on your resume or LinkedIn profile to demonstrate what a great dad, brother, spouse, friend or coworker you've been. In other words, because it can't be measured, you rarely prioritize building relationships.

In addition, another reason you put relationships on the back burner is that there are so many seemingly great excuses for doing so. Many argue that all of their hard work is necessary so that their family can enjoy the perfect life. Or, there's also the classic, "I'll spend more time with the people I love as soon as I make partner, sell my company, pay off my second home, etc." Neither of these arguments makes sense because that perfect life doesn't often include *you,* and you know what will happen as soon as you make partner: you'll just keep working the way you are working now.

Life is *Only* About Relationships

Like you, I've spent too much of my adult life believing that relationships would take care of themselves without much attention from me. I was convinced that I should commit the majority of my time towards achieving recognition as a talented professional – that is, building the impressive resume.

I knew that relationships were important, but I wasn't prepared to commit a meaningful amount of time and effort towards their development. This view has changed over time as I began to explore what I needed to do in order to feel more satisfaction and happiness in my own life.

I was heavily influenced by a psychologist with long hair named Greg Sipes. Dr. Sipes is the managing partner in one of the largest mental health practices in the Midwest. Since 1994, he's been my counselor, business partner, mentor and friend. His insight is extremely valuable because over the past thirty-plus years, he has worked with hundreds of extremely successful professionals who for one reason or another feel that something is missing in their life.

As you might imagine, Dr. Sipes believes that it's important to build meaningful relationships. However, he goes one very important step further, arguing that life is *only* about relationships. He believes (and research supports) that as long as an individual has access to the basic necessities (food, shelter, health, satellite radio), he or she has the same ability to feel satisfaction and happiness as the wealthiest person on the planet. The only factor that can ensure that they enjoy this fulfillment is the quality of their relationships.

His conviction is based on thousands of hours sitting with overachieving professionals who have the same characteristics. They are wealthy, sit at the top of their professions and have more stuff than they could ever need. Unfortunately, many of the talented professionals who visit Dr. Sipes are extremely unhappy and dissatisfied with their accomplishments. In most cases, these individuals have a history of unhealthy relationships in their lives.

Since Dr. Sipes helped me understand the strong connection between healthy relationships and a person's happiness, I began to wonder if this theory was true of the people who I was trying to help gain clarity in their businesses. Was the satisfaction of overachieving professionals tied to satisfaction in their personal lives? Because I spend my entire week dealing with these types of people, my business provides the ideal environment to test this hypothesis.

I began to consider how satisfied each of my clients (current and past) was with their life, both personally and professionally. I thought about the individuals who made more money than they could ever spend and lived in huge homes but who rarely felt satisfied with their accomplishments. On the opposite end of the spectrum, I had clients who drove old cars and made a very average amount of money, but who never seemed to have a bad day. I began to recognize that there was very little connection between a client's financial success and their happiness.

One thing became crystal clear: The professionals who believed that making tons of money, earning more recognition, or having the nicest "stuff" was going to make them happy, never felt satisfied – no matter what they achieved. They kept setting and achieving impressive goals, but unless they had healthy relationships, the contentment they were hoping to find never materialized. Money really can't buy happiness.

I'd be surprised if any of this is a giant revelation to you or any other overachiever reading this book. If you reflect back on your life, the moments when you suffered the most pain or happiness were probably associated with the people you care about the most. You might remember the day you landed the "big account," bought your first luxury car or got a promotion. However, none of these events stir up the same emotions as when you think about your wedding day, the birth of your first child, or the loss of a close relative.

The undeniable truth is that we are wired by our creator to be social and to build meaningful relationships with other people. Without these, life is empty no matter whatever else you achieve. Or as Dr. Sipes points out, "Life is *only* about relationships."

The Problem With Resolutions

I can imagine how you're feeling. You recognize there's a problem and understand that addressing the issue isn't all that complex. Unfortunately, just like someone who's spent years making unfulfilled New Year's resolutions to lose weight, to you the challenge probably seems overwhelming. It's too easy to reflect back on the many times you've tried and failed to find the time to work on your relationships.

I get it, it's tough. But, I'm 100% certain that you are capable of making the changes necessary to build meaningful relationships. Like all overachievers, you just need a plan, a way to measure your progress, and some momentum to get you going. It's not enough to write someone's name on a Post It® note and stick it on your bathroom mirror, hoping that you'll magically find opportunities to hang out and "bond." You've got to be intentional about this effort or eventually most of the "build relationships" activity will get pushed to the bottom of your to-do list. If you're truly committed to change, the following process will help you to reprioritize your behavior around what really matters: the people who mean the most to you and who make life worth living.

Name Your MIPs (Most Important People)

Before you sign up to coach your kid's soccer team or become a Den mother, I'd advise you to slow down and get crystal clear about *who* it is that really needs your attention. This should be relatively easy, but just in case it isn't, I would consider the following: close family, close friends, peers/employees from work with whom you spend a bunch of time. That's it. Don't overthink this piece or you'll never get started. You can always add someone later.

Once you've got the list of your MIPs, the real work begins. Remember, working on tasks that are difficult to measure and rarely deliver immediate gratification is difficult. I've found that the best way to keep this activity a priority in my busy life is to first come up with a detailed picture of the type of impact I'd like to make on this group of special people. This has helped me to stay focused and create a process that delivers meaningful results.

The process for developing a clear picture is fairly straightforward. Pick one of the individuals on your list and imagine that they were asked to say a few words about you at your funeral, retirement party, or other important occasion. Visualize your spouse, best friend or coworker standing in front of a crowd and giving an emotional talk about the impact you made on their life. What would you want them to say? Actually write it down. Here's what I produced when I completed this exercise:

- **Spouse** - *CJ provided unconditional love and encouragement and was a strong leader who inspired me to be the best I could be.*

- **Best Friend(s)** - *CJ was always there for me. He helped me through my most difficult challenges and helped me achieve my biggest wins.*

- **Children** - *Dad taught me that I was a special, loved child of God who was capable of achieving any dream I could imagine.*

- **Community** - *CJ inspired us to believe in ourselves and push beyond our perceived limits.*

These simple phrases have helped me to stay committed to building strong relationships. It works because it acts as a compass that keeps me pointed in the right direction. It gives me something to measure my actions against, so I can judge how I am doing with my goal, and work to do better. It's a very powerful process that can inspire even the busiest professionals to refocus on the most important people in their lives.

About five years ago one of my closest friends from college lost his sister to cystic fibrosis. Her showing was on a Thursday evening between 5:00 and 8:00 p.m. in a northern suburb of Chicago, about a four-hour drive for me. That same day I had a speaking engagement that lasted until 4:00 p.m. and another commitment the next morning at 8:00 a.m. When I looked at the schedule for the day, I definitely had a moment where I thought *this is not all gonna happen*. But there was never a question in my mind about what I would prioritize: I would be there because Tom was one of the most important people in my life and I wanted him to feel that I was "always there for him." My written statement about what I wanted to be for my close friend guided my behavior. I jumped in the car after my speech, made it to the showing as it was closing, and then drove back to Indianapolis to get as much sleep as I could for the meeting the next morning. I was not at my sharpest that day, but I was 100% certain I made the right decision.

Don't panic if this exercise points out a disconnect between what would be said about you *today* and what you hope people will say about you *in the future*. For example, a husband may wish that his wife saw him as a loving provider who made time for their marriage, but recognizes that today she may feel that he's simply a guy who's obsessed with his work and rarely makes time for the family. This disconnect is completely normal. Rarely do individuals feel like their relationships are exactly where they'd like them to be when they first engage in this process. Personally, I needed (and continue to need) a lot of work to stay focused on building the types of relationships that I feel are the most important. This is especially true of my relationship with my kids, because I often tend to focus too heavily on their achievements and not as much on simply enjoying time with them.

Instead of worrying about your current situation, this exercise is designed to help you identify what you'd want these important people to say about you in the *future*. The resulting descriptions provide a clear vision of what your behavior needs to be in order to earn these kind words. In other words, you've got to begin with the end in mind.

After you've made your list, stand back and take a look at it. How does it make you feel to think about each of the individuals you've chosen and what you hope they will say about you? Unless you're a robot, this quiet reflection should stir many powerful emotions – some good (those relationships that are healthy) and some bad (those that you've neglected for a long time). Either way, you're beginning to see the essential role these people play in your life. In case you're not completely sold on the idea that "life is only about relationships," I'd like to challenge you to list the five priorities in life (other than your health, because that is a given we all share) that are *more* important to you than the most important people in your life. I'd be surprised if you can identify *any* priorities that are more important to you than the people on this list.

Before moving on, I'd first like to congratulate you for completing this effort. You are now a member of a small group of professionals who have actually taken the time to narrow down the hundreds of people you know to a concise list of those who are the most important. In addition, you've gained clarity around the type of relationship you'd like to have with each one. Focusing on building close, meaningful relationships with everyone is impossible – remember, if everything is important, nothing is important. This clarity will be extremely helpful in deciding how you prioritize your time outside the office.

Actions to Back Up Your Intentions

Clarifying your intention to build stronger relationships is a great start but as Jordan Belfort, the "Wolf of Wall Street," pointed out, "Without action the best intentions in the world are nothing more than that: intentions."[xvi] In other words, it's time to get to work.

At this point in the journey, it will be tempting to send out a mass email to the people on your list proudly declaring that things are going to change! You now recognize that you've been extremely selfish and it's time to become a much better friend, son/daughter, spouse, father/mother and church member. You'll pick up the phone, set up meetings and promise to begin spending more time with everyone.

I highly discourage this approach. First, you're going to sound a little silly and everyone will assume something's wrong with you. Do you remember how everyone responded to Jerry Maguire's memo? It didn't go so well. In addition, when your commitment to this endeavor dissipates (which it will in approximately seven days) all you'll be left with is a big "promise" that included zero specifics and is soon forgotten by everybody – including yourself.

You've been doing it your way for a lot of years and no matter how inspiring these words might be, no book can ever lead to a complete reversal in behavior. Instead, I suggest that you imagine you're walking out into a rough ocean. Instead of running into the biggest wave, I'd like you to wade slowly into this next phase in your journey.

Here's how that process looks.

As you do with any big goal, you should break it down into its smallest components. In doing this, the initial task you should

---

xvi   Jordan Belfort, *The Wolf of Wall Street* (New York: Bantam, 2007).

undertake is to rank the list. I'm not really concerned with who lands in each spot, but I do want to make sure that we can all agree that your very closest family members need to be your initial focus. That doesn't mean that the others go on the back burner, but I'd rather you not schedule a week-long golfing trip with your buddies before agreeing to attend most of your son's baseball games. Make sense?

Next, the simplest, easiest, and most obvious place to start on this journey is to begin by spending more *time* with the people you love. Buying them big gifts will never replace the bond you develop in intimate situations where real conversations take place. As I mentioned above, it's not enough to simply announce "I'm going to spend more time with you!" You've got to implement a tactic/process to ensure it actually occurs.

I know from experience that in an extremely hectic and busy life, it's nearly impossible to find the time for anything that doesn't grow your business or have an immediate benefit. Here's an extremely complex solution I've instituted to ensure that I make time to strengthen these relationships: I actually schedule it right on the calendar. That's right, I open up Google Calendar, set an appointment and invite the other party to ensure it gets on their schedule.

Putting it in the calendar is simple; making sure neither I nor the other individual(s) attending don't cancel it can be challenging. In order to make certain these meetings take place, I have a couple of tactics I use. First, I get the person to make a commitment up front, telling them that if there's any chance at all they'll cancel then we shouldn't agree to the meeting. Next, I remind them the day before, indicating how much I'm looking forward to the meeting – even if I'm not. Finally, I plan for the meeting and make certain I do my part to make this a valuable use of our time.

In practice, the process is always a little trickier to execute. About six years ago, I was beginning to realize that being a dad and husband was a far more difficult challenge than I had expected. I needed some help beyond all the "how to raise your kids" books on my shelf. I wanted to talk to other dads and see how they were handling these issues. I started a group called the *"Purpose Driven Dads."* Initially, we met monthly and all were welcome. We did this for about one year and soon found out that the attendance was sporadic at best, and because new people showed up every time, it was near impossible to develop any meaningful connections. So, I scrapped the idea.

With this experience fresh in my memory, I decided to try a different approach. I handpicked six guys who were at similar places in their lives – they had young kids, lived near me and had busy schedules. Next, I twisted their arms and got them all to agree to meet weekly at the same place, same time (Friday, 7:30 a.m., Bob Evans). In more than a year, we've developed extremely open and close relationships that have benefitted us all. It wasn't easy, but because I was crystal clear about the *who* and the *why*, I kept pushing past all the obstacles to make it happen.

I also wanted to improve the relationship with my son. I thought it was important to create memories that would shape the kind of man he would become. I didn't know where to start. *Should I take him on a hike across the Rocky Mountains? Maybe I could teach him how to fish?* Unfortunately, I'm not much of an outdoorsman and my ten-year-old son didn't seem all that interested in a weeklong bonding experience with just his dad. After some brainstorming, I got the breakfast group together and convinced them that we should take our kids on a three-day excursion that summer where we would fish, hike, eat a ton, goof off and talk about what's really important in life.

Again, this was anything but easy. It was nearly impossible to find three days in the summer in between vacations and travel sports schedules. But, we did it – selecting weekdays instead of weekends – and I'm pleased to announce that we just successfully completed our fourth trip. It's become a tradition that we all look forward to more than anything else.

As you can imagine, the ideas for scheduling these types of events are limitless. It could be as simple as a weekly date night with your spouse or a weeklong golfing trip to Ireland with your dad. It doesn't matter what it is, just make certain that it gets on your schedule and remains a priority – no matter what else comes up!

Another benefit of this behavior is that once you get in the habit of scheduling these events, you will begin to see their value in strengthening relationships with everyone in your life, not just those who made your list. The perfect place to test this out is in the workplace. In every office, we've all got a handful of peers who are critical to our success. Even if you may not love these individuals, I suggest that you schedule regular interactions with them to have a meaningful conversation about how things are going – even if it's trivial in nature. This type of critical and predictable contact builds trust and if you're lucky, friendship.

Scheduling regular meetings, phone calls or even vacations with the most important people in your life isn't the only way to strengthen these relationships (nor is it practical in many instances). There's another unbelievably simple strategy that I've found useful: show gratitude to others on a regular basis. That's it – just be grateful for the impact someone else has made on your life.

The Power of Gratitude

Gratitude is an unbelievably powerful way to improve relationships because in today's hectic, fast-paced society, very few people take the time to be truly thankful. We send short text/email messages with "THX" and assume the message has been delivered. As a result, sincere appreciation has become a precious commodity.

Think about it for a second, how many examples can you recall when someone took the time to let you know how much they appreciated your efforts? I've asked this question hundreds of times and rarely do I find someone who can remember more than a handful of instances. In fact, many men can't remember *even one time* when they were shown genuine appreciation from someone else.

Gratitude is a rare and powerful tool for building the types of relationships that add satisfaction and joy to your life. Unfortunately, for most people (especially men) it doesn't come naturally. You're too busy "accomplishing" to slow down and think about the positive impact others are making in your life, much less take the time to send them a quick note.

I'm no different from you. I work hard, both personally and professionally, and expect others to do the same. Rarely are my efforts recognized by others and that's OK. Consequently, it was hard for me to imagine that others needed to be appreciated.

But they do, and as I've found over the years, so do I. In fact, I thrive on it.

Gratitude can be delivered in many different shapes and sizes: handwritten notes, gifts, public praise, etc. I don't think that the method matters nearly as much as the intent and the effort. In other words, a "nice work" every couple of months to your employees, friends and family may not be enough.

Nearly ten years ago, I began to intentionally work at being grateful towards the people in my life. It started on New Year's day when I was running through a list of "resolutions" I was considering for the upcoming year. I remember flipping through the bowl games and thinking *I never follow through on these commitments – I wonder if there is something that I could do immediately to build some momentum?*

The next thing I knew, I had pulled out some notecards and was writing a message to my closest friends. In each one, I thanked them for the unique impact they had made in my life over the years. I reflected back on great memories and made certain they knew that because of their friendship I was a better person. I've continued this New Year's tradition ever since.

For the females reading this book, please understand something: guys don't send heartfelt notes. It's just not what we do. We say "thanks" by purchasing a case of beer or single malt scotch. That's why this gesture (which some of my more sarcastic friends refer to as a "love letter") is so unique and impactful. It stands out and makes an impression. It helps me to build the types of relationships that make my life better.

In the years since I started this annual tradition, I've continued working hard at being thankful with everyone in my life and believe it or not, it's become much easier. I'm now on the lookout to recognize people who probably don't hear it enough because I understand the positive impression it can make. For example, at the end-of-year meetings with teachers, I always include a somewhat long-winded speech (which usually irritates my wife Nicole) about how important their efforts are to the development of my children.

Be Honest About Your Capacity to Engage

In case you're wondering, this effort does takes time, but not nearly as much as you think. While I do focus on being kinder and more grateful to everyone in my life, especially those who I interact with on a regular basis (teachers, coaches, pastor, etc.), I don't try and develop a close relationship with everyone. You can't develop strong, meaningful relationships with every single acquaintance in your life – there simply aren't enough hours in the day.

While I will concede that it's probably different for everyone, I don't believe that you can effectively build and nurture more than a half dozen close relationships outside of your family. These are the types of friends that you'll work hard to earn the following praise: "CJ was always there for me. He helped me through my most difficult challenges and helped me achieve my biggest wins."

If you do try to build this type of relationship with too many people, you'll end up frustrated with your efforts and you'll have people assuming that you're not a very good friend. You've probably got a few contacts that you see every couple of years, each time agreeing that "we've got to get together more often," only to ignore them until the next chance encounter. This point was driven home many years ago when I ran into a friend of mine from college. Moments after I threw out the obligatory, "Let's hook up soon," he had the courage to say, "CJ, let's be honest, we're both busy right now, let's just not agree to something we both know won't happen." It was truly cathartic.

Understanding what makes you unique and spending more of your time engaging these qualities is an important piece of the "success" puzzle. Committing the resources to build meaningful, loving relationships is another. However, neither of these efforts will work if all you're trying to do is add a handful of additional accomplishments to your resume. The final step in this equation – *enjoying the journey* – ensures that you'll appreciate the happiness and satisfaction you always assumed success would bring.

Three Key Points to Remember

1. We spend the majority of our waking hours on activities that generate measurable results. This almost never includes spending quality time with the people that mean the most to us: family and close friends.

2. Life is only about relationships. As long as you have the means to provide for your basic necessities, you can be as content as anyone on the planet. The key to your satisfaction and happiness past this point is directly related to the quality of the relationships with the people you love.

3. Deep down you know it's important to improve these relationships, but for a number of reasons, you've never made it a priority. This will only change if you commit to the following:

   ° Identify the five-to-eight most valuable people in your life. You may have a ton of friends but not a ton of time to make them all a priority. As Patrick Lencioni pointed out, "*If everything is important, then nothing is.*"[xvii]

   ° Develop and implement specific strategies for clearly demonstrating the value these people bring to your life. In other words, be *intentional*.

---

xvii   Patrick Lencioni, "If everything is important...," The Table Group, March 2006, accessed March 13, 2017, https://www.tablegroup.com/blog/if-everything-is-important.

Chapter 4 – Taking Action

Life is only about relationships. We all know this, but as we learned in this chapter, very few people actually prioritize the most important people in their lives.

In this exercise, I'm going to help you get a jump start on building the meaningful relationships that will bring more joy and contentment to your life. Here's how this works:

1. Select at least three extremely important relationships that today don't get as much attention as you would like.

2. Brainstorm and list two different strategies for strengthening each of these bonds. As you do this, remember that there are only so many hours in the day – in other words, don't overdo it!

You can complete this exercise in the space below or by downloading a template at CoachCJ.com/bookexercises.

Relationship	Strategy #1	Strategy #2
Corinne: 10-year-old daughter	Bi-weekly breakfasts	Overnight summer trip.

	Relationship	Strategy #1	Strategy #2
1			
2			
3			
4			
5			

CHAPTER 5

Smell the Roses

"Enjoy the journey because the destination is a mirage."
— Steven Furtick

When I reflect back on the hundreds of professionals I've worked with over the years, many truths are self-evident. One of the clearest is this: from the outside looking in, their lives appear almost perfect. They excelled through high school, earned exceptional grades in college, landed the perfect job upon finishing their studies and quickly advanced in their profession. Nearly all would admit that they have achieved more than they could have imagined in their early twenties.

The statistics bear out this perception. If you were to compare these individuals to the rest of the world, here's what you'd find:

- Their household income is greater than 95% of families in the U.S., which easily places them in the top 1% globally.

- They live in large homes, drive nice cars, and take great vacations.

- From a material standpoint, they lack almost nothing and rarely put off a purchase simply because it's expensive.

It is interesting to note that each of these professionals followed the same strategy to achieve success: set an ambitious goal, work extremely hard, reach the objective, and then quickly move on to the next milestone. This approach always delivers proven, measurable results year in and year out. Typical overachieving professionals (you, me, most of our friends and peers) assume there's no reason to change a thing.

As I said, from the outside looking in, life seems perfect.

However, as you know by now, life doesn't always feel as perfect as it looks. Like most of my clients, you're probably wondering if all the money, recognition and stuff is worth all the hard work if you never seem to enjoy the journey. Worse, you probably assume that you're the only person feeling this way because everybody else seems to be so happy.

I promise – you're not alone. The majority of the people who appear to be completely satisfied with their lives feel the same worries and doubts as you do, but like you, they all assume the best path forward is to do what they have been doing and maintain the illusion that life is perfect.

I used to feel exactly the same way. That was until I began coaching highly accomplished professionals who seemed to have it all figured out – both personally and professionally. I soon recognized that these people all shared a similar challenge: no matter what they achieved, it never seemed to be enough.

Early in my business, I had a client whose path illustrated this story, which I've seen repeated hundreds of times over the years. He was a successful executive in his early fifties with an impressive background, whose hard work resulted in an extremely fast career ascension. His efforts earned him the respect of his peers, multiple three thousand dollar suits and more than $400,000 per year in income.

Soon after we began working together, it became clear that one goal was far more important to him than all the rest. My client was convinced that as soon as he earned half a million dollars a year, everything else would fall into place. This achievement would lead to the type of recognition, lifestyle, and financial freedom that would make him finally feel successful.

Less than a year later, after a ton of effort, he surpassed the $500,000 mark by nearly sixty thousand dollars. At this early stage in my career, I had never seen anyone hit such an ambitious goal so quickly. I was excited to be a part of this journey and couldn't wait to help him celebrate this important milestone at our next meeting. My enthusiasm lasted all of about sixty minutes. Despite a near record improvement in revenue, by the end of our meeting, my client was already on to the next goal: $650,000. It just so happened that this figure was twenty-five thousand more than the amount one of his peers had just earned.

I wish I could tell you that my brilliant coaching was able to provide some much-needed perspective and that he learned to appreciate his success. Unfortunately, that wasn't the case. Over the next few years, his "never enough" cycle repeated itself over and over again.

I distinctly remember one conversation revolving around a golf weekend he had completed with some friends from his country club. The group rented a house on the ocean near a handful of luxurious courses. They played three rounds, ate at the best restaurants and finished off each evening smoking cigars on a large, elevated deck overlooking the Atlantic.

I assumed my client would return from this trip excited to provide me a handful of amazing highlights from the weekend: golf stories and great moments with his buddies. I was wrong. Instead, we spent more than an hour discussing the "mistakes" he had made throughout his career, which had led to an average income, no real assets, and a dismal future which would require him to work until he was sixty. Sure enough, there were a couple of guys on the golf trip who owned successful companies and had really "made it." They had bigger homes, nicer cars and no longer needed to go to the office each day. They spent their time taking lavish vacations, buying great new toys and of course, lowering their handicap.

Despite his own success, my client simply couldn't get past the fact that in his opinion, he had peers who'd accomplished significantly more. He understood that his income and professional accomplishments clearly placed him in the top 1%, but it didn't seem to make a difference, because there would always be others who had done better. I could tell that this frustration consumed his thoughts and kept him from enjoying anything in his life.

That was the moment I began to develop the next – and most critical – part of my coaching strategy: an action plan for actually enjoying your success.

You're Close, But Still Not There

Developing a clear idea of the skills and abilities that make you different is important. It will help you gently guide your personal and professional life in a direction that more effectively utilizes your unique talents.

Understanding the importance of your most valuable relationships will change your life. It should influence your priorities in a way that will focus more of your time and energy towards the people you love.

In theory, making these two subtle shifts in the way you approach life should deliver the satisfaction and happiness you've been searching for all these years. Unfortunately, I've rarely seen it work out that way. The reason is that knowing what to do and doing it are at opposite ends of the spectrum. You've been doing it your way for a long time and no matter how compelling you found the first four chapters of this book, it's unlikely that becoming exposed to the truth will lead to a massive change in your behavior.

Sorry, I wish I was that good. If simply exposing someone to the answer was all it took, there would never be another diet/exercise book or video ever released. The marriage counseling business would cease to exist, personal trainers wouldn't get another client, and I would probably have to go out and find a real job. Understanding what to do is fairly easy; doing it is typically really, really hard.

My point is that change is going to take time. No matter what any chiseled stud tells you in an infomercial, you're not going to lose weight working out eleven minutes a day, three days a week. And the guy promising that if you just buy his book, you'll make at least $100,000 a year flipping houses working from home, in your pajamas, in less than ten hours a week, is full of shit.

It doesn't work that way. Meaningful change takes time.

The truth is that for the rest of your life, you will always be working at becoming a better friend/spouse/parent/child/leader/etc. In addition, I recommend that you wake up every day and ask yourself if you could possibly utilize your unique abilities more effectively in the next twenty-four hours. This book isn't about a destination, it's about a journey, one that doesn't end until you do.

Let that sink in for a second.

You're on a journey of introspection and self-improvement. No matter how hard you work, how many workshops you attend or how many books you read, you will never wake up one day and declare, "I've done it! There's no reason to improve. Life is perfect and from this moment forward, every second will be filled with complete bliss and happiness." You're either getting better or getting worse, there's no such thing as "maintaining the status quo."

You can view this situation in one of two ways. First, you could decide to go through life frustrated that's there's no magical time where you "arrive" at complete satisfaction. Or, you could choose to figure out the best way to enjoy the journey. Either way, it's your call.

Once I came to the realization that my life was a grand expedition to be experienced rather than a contest to win, I began to see everything differently. I dialed down (not eliminated, I'm still a work in progress) my obsession with results and begin instead to actually appreciate the process – even when it was painful. Since then, I've been focused on finding the best practices for helping the overachieving professional feel this same peace and happiness. While there are certainly dozens of tactics that can help you enjoy the journey, I've narrowed it down to the following four that I've seen have the greatest impact.

1. Live in the Moment

You probably like this book, or you would have set it down by now and considered posting a negative review on Amazon. Some of the ideas might have really hit home, and if I've done my job, you may have already recommended it to a friend. (If you haven't already done so, please feel free to set the book down and post an amazing review on all of your social outlets. Go ahead, I'll wait, no hurry.)

However, no matter how compelling this message, if you're like me, and most overachievers on this planet, you probably struggle to get through more than a few paragraphs in a book without your mind drifting off and thinking about something else. In fact, I'm certain that more than once while reading this book you've gotten to the bottom of the page and wondered, "Wait – what was he talking about?"

Don't panic, you're not crazy, this is completely normal. The truth is that you're wired to chase success, and up until this point that meant achievement. As a result, it's nearly impossible for your brain to focus on the current moment for very long because it's too busy thinking about what you've got to do next or regretting past mistakes you might have made. Thus, you drift off in the middle of reading a book, listening to a speaker or watching you kid's soccer game.

Here's the problem with this inability to live in the moment: it will keep you from enjoying the journey. In fact, this obsession with the past and the future is the cause of virtually all of the stress and anxiety you feel, according to Harvard psychologist Daniel Gilbert. He argues that we tend to poorly remember the past, and then utilize this information to inaccurately predict the future.[xviii] Unfortunately, many overachievers tend to err on the negative side when we reflect and predict.

Consider the following example. You're sitting in a long meeting and find yourself thinking about the challenging month you've had at work. You worked long hours, made a few mistakes and found yourself in multiple uncomfortable conversations with your peers. You feel frustrated, and it doesn't appear that the workload is going to let up any time soon. As you look out toward tomorrow, next week and even next month, you start feeling depressed, assuming that every day will be filled with the exact same emotions you're experiencing right now.

One of the best ways to enjoy the journey is to resist this urge to worry about how you might "feel" tomorrow or regret mistakes you've made in the past. Instead, do your very best to keep your attention exclusively on this moment and accept the present exactly as it is, not as you wish it would be. Chasing a different reality than the one that currently exists is a recipe for a lifetime filled with stress and unhappiness.

Live in the moment without judgement. It really is that simple. However, simple doesn't mean easy. Don't expect to make this change in perspective and behavior overnight. It goes against everything you've been taught since childhood and seems to defy the basic fundamentals of what it takes to be successful. However, I give you my word, this simple practice will help you feel more satisfaction in your life – both personally and professionally. In

xviii   Daniel Gilbert, *Stumbling on Happiness* (New York: Vintage Books, 2007).

addition, the clarity of mind you'll begin to enjoy will lead to better decision making and improved results.

So, how do you calm your mind in a world filled with deadlines, competition and constant information overload? As I mentioned, it isn't easy and will take some time. But with practice you can learn to focus on the here and now. I've been working on this for several years and have a handful of thoughts to get you started.

First, unlike every other achievement in your life, you can't master this practice by laying out a plan and working really hard through a variety of steps leading toward an end result. It doesn't work that way. At the core, what you're doing is focusing your awareness on nothing but the current environment you're experiencing. That's it – nothing more. I know that the overachiever in you is very doubtful that "doing nothing" is a viable strategy.

Because your brain thinks it's absolutely nuts to focus on the present when you could be so much more productive by doing at least three things at once, you need to train it to come back to the moment when it begins to drift. You've got to build up your awareness "muscle" or you'll forever be chasing the next distraction. Here's a few exercises to start your training regimen.

Since college, I've struggled with anxiety and depression. Initially, I was absolutely certain that I needed to "fight" this affliction. Like any overachiever, I completed a boatload of therapy and read all the self-help books in an effort to control my condition. I believed that any anxious or sad thoughts should be labeled as "bad" and must be vanquished immediately. It's as though I was building a moat around my mind, trusting that the deeper and wider, the better.

If I've learned anything in dealing with this challenge it's this: "what you resist, persists." In other words, stop building the moat, because no matter what you do, you can't keep a thought from entering your brain. In fact, every ounce of effort you dedicate to "resisting" the thought only gives it more power. If you doubt me, try this exercise for one day: try not to think about something. I promise, twenty-four hours from now you'll realize that it simply doesn't work.

The first exercise in the "live in the moment" training program is to accept all thoughts that enter your mind with as little judgment as possible. Once an idea pops into your head that you dislike, recognize it and then simply let it go. This is very different than analyzing an idea and trying to keep it from ever coming back again. Intellectually, this is extremely simple. However, learning to observe and release your thoughts is like trying to play tennis with your non-dominant hand: it's very awkward at first and takes a long time to become a habit.

Another great exercise that will help you to be more self-aware of your present circumstances and less obsessed with the past/future is meditation. When I mention this practice to most professionals, they look at me like I've lost my mind. The idea of meditating probably conjures up an image of a monk sitting on the floor of a sparsely furnished monastery, eyes closed, listening to bells chiming in the far off distance.

I'm well aware that the idea of sitting around and doing nothing seems crazy. But, just like going to the driving range to lower your handicap, meditation is a great method for training your mind to slow down and focus on the "now." Developing this habit reduces the onslaught of ideas that bombard your conscious by simply increasing the space between thoughts.

Like the first exercise of learning to accept and release your negative thoughts, learning to meditate is straightforward, but can be extremely difficult to turn into a regular practice. I've been mediating for years and it's common for me to get a few minutes into a session and wonder if I can stop "thinking" for even ten seconds.

But I promise that it works. In addition to helping you become more self-aware of the present, the physical and psychological benefits are well-researched and documented. They include less stress, better concentration and decision making, improved cardiovascular and immune health and more happiness in your daily life.

Before starting this practice, I want you to understand that there's no right or wrong way to meditate. Unlike everything else you've achieved in your life, there's no use in laying out a plan because there's no official destination. This is a journey; you can't measure the results in Microsoft Excel, and there's no recognition for being the best.

I began many years ago by turning off the lights in my office, putting on headphones with relaxing music and sitting quietly for a few minutes each morning. I then moved on to a formal practice called Transcendental Meditation (TM) which helped me to increase my commitment to the habit. Since then, I've tried a handful of apps, including the popular Headspace. Every one of these tactics has provided different benefits. My advice is simple: experiment with a few different methods until you find one that seems to fit you the best, recognizing that, like your workout routine at the gym, this practice will constantly evolve.

2. Be Grateful

If you're reading this, chances are good that you're filthy rich. Let me describe your day:

- You woke to an alarm and rolled out of a comfortable bed.
- You took a hot shower, brushed your teeth and ate a healthy breakfast.
- You got into a car equipped with heat and AC.
- You went to a well-appointed office with electricity, a desk and even great snacks.
- You're going to eat a nice dinner and then probably watch TV on the couch before you go to bed.

With that in mind, consider these facts:

- 1.4 billion people on the planet live on less than $1.25 per day.
- 1.7 billion people lack access to clean water.
- 22 million children die each day because of malnutrition.

The understatement of the day is this: we are blessed. Unfortunately, most people, especially overachieving professionals, focus on what they lack, rather than on their good fortune. This perspective makes it nearly impossible to really enjoy the journey.

Much like being in the moment, living gratefully is a simple choice that shapes how you interpret every piece of information you absorb on a daily basis. As I mentioned in the previous chapter, gratitude is powerful. A grateful person tends to see everything in a positive light, while the pessimist always finds something wrong. The glass is truly half empty or half full.

I'm not the first person to bring this to your attention. You've known someone who's lost a loved one, struggled to find a job or gone through a terrible divorce. Every time you reflect on these difficult situations, you momentarily count your blessings, recognizing that you've got it good. Unfortunately, this perspective only lasts for a short period of time. Before you know it, you're back to playing the comparison game, wondering how in the world your neighbor can afford a new boat.

Why is it so hard to focus on our abundance rather than our shortcomings? As I mentioned in Chapter One, we've been wired from an early age to believe that the only way to feel "successful" is through constant achievement and recognition. This approach leads to the belief that stopping to be grateful is a waste of time when there's so much left to accomplish.

The problem is made worse by the non-stop messages we get from the marketplace. In his book *Buyology*, Martin Lindstrom points out that the majority of advertising in the world today is focused on the emotion of fear. Companies have known for a long time that the best way to grow is by convincing you that your life is incomplete, empty, horrible, etc. without their products. He argues that this "fear-based" advertising plays "less on our generalized anxieties and more on our insecurities about ourselves."[xix] If you've ever bought something you didn't really need

---

xix   Martin Lindstrom, *Buyology: Truth and Lies About Why We Buy* (New York: Broadway Books, 2010), 199.

(watch, car, shirt, vacation home, etc.) then you know exactly how persuasive this message can be.

Living gratefully is extremely difficult. Your upbringing, competitive peers and non-stop "you're not good enough" message from the marketplace make it almost impossible to focus on everything good in your life. Despite this uphill battle, developing a grateful perspective is essential if you're interested in enjoying the journey. As Melody Beattie said in probably my favorite quote of all time:

> *Gratitude unlocks the fullness of life. It turns what we have into enough, and more. It turns denial into acceptance, chaos to order, confusion to clarity. It can turn a meal into a feast, a house into a home, a stranger into a friend. Gratitude makes sense of our past, brings peace for today and creates a vision for tomorrow.*[xx]

Like any meaningful change in perspective, focusing on what you've got instead of what you don't takes time. I've been working at it for years and found a handful of regular practices that help strengthen my gratitude "muscle."

- *Daily Reminder* – Staying focused on anything, especially something like gratitude, which is nearly impossible to measure, isn't easy. That's why you need something to keep this concept at the top of your mind on a regular basis. The options for making this happen are almost limitless (set a phone alarm, Post It® Note on your PC, hire me to call you

---

xx   "Melody Beattie Quotes," Goodreads, accessed March 13, 2017, https://www.goodreads.com/author/quotes/4482.Melody_Beattie

every two hours, etc.). Having tried just about everything, I recommend something permanent that you look at all the time and other people will ask you about – a picture on the wall, a marble/glass paperweight, etc. I remind myself by keeping a small pebble near my monitor that has the word "Grace" engraved on the front.

- *Gratitude Journal* – Keep a journal document of everything in life for which you are grateful. Research shows that simply identifying five items each week makes a significant positive impact on both your physical and psychological well-being. I suggest that you try and pick something specific and unique each day. For example, right now I am grateful that I have a warm office when it's fifteen degrees outside. You can keep this journal on your phone or computer, in a beautiful leather book or in a $1.99 spiral bound notebook left over from your kid's middle school English class. The format doesn't matter; the action does.

- *Thank You Notes* – Several years ago, I was sitting around the house on New Year's Day feeling extremely grateful for the meaningful relationships I have in my life. I did something crazy and wrote a handwritten letter to my closest friends – a tradition that I've kept up ever since. This practice has spilled over into many other relationships and I've found that writing personal notes always reminds me that I'm so blessed to have amazing, caring and loving people in my life. Go buy some "thank you" notes and set aside twenty minutes to write one card today – you'll be amazed at how good it makes you feel – not to mention the person who receives it.

3. Give Generously

As previously discussed, most overachieving professionals are wealthy and rarely, if ever, go without. We have everything we need and more. Unfortunately, not everyone is as lucky. In addition to the global statistics mentioned earlier, consider these 2015 figures representing the challenges in the United States:[xxi]

- 43.1 million people (13.5 percent) lived in poverty.

- 24.4 million (12.4 percent) of people ages 18-64 lived in poverty.

- 14.5 million (19.7 percent) children under the age of 18 lived in poverty.

- 4.2 million (8.8 percent) seniors 65 and older lived in poverty.

- 42.2 million Americans lived in food insecure households, including 29.1 million adults and 13.1 million children.

- 13 percent of households (15.8 million households) were food insecure.

These statistics should be alarming to everyone reading this book. Americans live in the one of the wealthiest country on the planet[xxii] and yet more than 13% of the population lives in pov-

---

xxi   "Hunger and Poverty Facts and Statistics," Feeding America, accessed March 15, 2017, http://www.feedingamerica.org/hunger-in-america/impact-of-hunger/hunger-and-poverty/hunger-and-poverty-fact-sheet.html.
xxii   Jonathan Gregson, "The Richest Countries in the World," Global Finance Magazine, February 13, 2017, https://www.gfmag.com/global-data/economic-data/richest-countries-in-the-world?page=12.

erty and nearly sixteen million households are uncertain if they're going to have enough food to eat on a regular basis.

At the highest level, this problem shouldn't be nearly this bad. Those of us who have more than we need should share with those who don't – it's that simple. The wealth we accumulate above what we need is far more than necessary to eliminate poverty and hunger in the U.S. for good.

Sadly, the average American donates less than 3% of his or her annual income to charitable organizations. While I don't claim to be an expert in poverty or non-profits, my experience dealing with thousands of professionals for more than thirteen years has provided some insight into why our giving is so low. Most overachieving professionals have convinced themselves that if they give too much, they'll run out and won't be able to provide for themselves and their families.

We argue that we'll donate more of our time and money as soon as we have enough. This, as you can imagine, is complete horseshit. Not only do we have plenty right now, we will almost always increase our definition of "enough" as our income grows. I once had a client who earned more than $700,000 a year tell me that money was too tight to donate at this time. Seriously, I can't make this stuff up.

Ending poverty and hunger is a great reason to reevaluate your personal budget and set aside more for charitable giving. But that's not why I challenge you to give generously. I'm encouraging you to donate more of your resources to those who are less fortunate for completely selfish reasons – it makes you feel better and significantly improves the likelihood that you will enjoy the journey.

Deep down, you know I'm right. Every time you do something nice for someone else, you feel great. You never write a check to a non-profit or spend time volunteering for a wonderful cause and then regret your decision – never (unless you were hammered at a black tie event and bid $7,500 for tickets to a basketball game). For most people, in fact, the good feelings we get from giving far outweigh the joy experienced when we're "getting" more for ourselves. About seven or eight years ago, I began to wonder if there was any science that backed up my theory that there was a significant psychological upside to "giving." After only a little exploration, I came across many studies that supported this belief, including compelling research from Dr. Stephen Post, a professor at Stony Brook University School of Medicine.

Dr. Post is recognized as a leader in studying the significant health benefits of helping others. His book, *Why Good Things Happen to Good People: How to Live a Longer, Healthier, Happier Life by the Simple Act of Giving*, inspired me to make helping those who are less fortunate an integral part of my coaching and speaking. The book is based on research from many of the nation's top universities (including a fifty-year study) clearly revealing that giving more of ourselves leads to a happier life, better physical health, less depression, increased good fortune and even a longer life. In other words, giving generously helps you to enjoy the journey.

But, just like living in the moment and being grateful, this simple concept is extremely difficult for most professionals to put into practice. It's one thing to donate $50 to help your nephew go on a mission trip. It's quite another to give your church bank routing information so they can automatically deduct a monthly contribution from your account. Giving generously requires a belief that you will always have plenty of resources to fulfill your needs. It means that you will prioritize putting the lives of others who are less fortunate above your perceived want to have another new suit, car, vacation, or even a nice dinner.

Shortly after reading this book and learning more about Dr. Post from the Institute for Research on Unlimited Love (www. UnlimitedLoveInstitute.org), I made a commitment to significantly increase my giving to organizations that benefitted those who were less fortunate. Since then, I've noticed a few things. First, I've never missed a penny of my charitable giving. More importantly, I've never felt happier or more satisfied with my life than when I'm giving in a meaningful way to others.

A quote published in the *Altoona Mirror* more than seventy years ago sums this up nicely: "We make a living by what we get, but we make a life by what we give."[xxiii] Trust me, your path to happiness has more to do with the impact you make on others than the content in your resume.

4. Consider Belief in a Higher Power

"It's not about you."

The first four words of Rick Warren's bestselling book, *The Purpose Drive Life* radically changed my thoughts about religon. Up until that point I was searching for the perfect church and pastor that could fulfill my spiritual "needs." I assumed that it was God's responsibility to make me happy. Unfortunately, no

---

xxiii "Mirrorgrams," *Altoona Mirror*, December 13, 1944.

matter how hard I looked, I was unable to find a perfect solution. That was until I realized that it wasn't about me.

I don't think that my existence is a random act of cosmic chance. I believe in a higher power that desperately wants me to live according to a handful of simple principles, including being grateful at all times for my blessings and generously giving of myself to others. Interestingly enough, when my life is aligned with these guidelines, I am happier, more satisfied and find it easier to enjoy the journey.

I believe this is by design. The God I believe in created me in His image and only he knows exactly what I need to do to get the most joy from this life. Looking back over the years, I can clearly see that the contentment I get from chasing worldly achievements (money, recognition, stuff) is fleeting and doesn't even come close to satisfaction I feel when living according to God's purpose.

I should probably mention that I'm a Christian, which among other things means that I believe the son of God (Jesus) came to Earth more than two thousand years ago. In addition, I also believe that he was crucified, suffered, died and was buried only to rise again three days later. I pray regularly, participate actively in a local church and do my very best to live according to the lessons from Jesus.

Having said that, my God doesn't instruct me to judge others who follow a different faith system. You won't ever see me jamming my religion down someone's throat – I'm not the guy on the airplane who spends the entire flight trying to "save" you. I respect all belief systems. In fact, I don't even think Jesus came to earth to start a religion. Rather, I believe that He came to teach us the best way to live, which at its core is focused on loving others.

I'm not interested in getting into a philosophical conversation about the existence of God – there are many others who do a much better job than I ever could. The point I'm making here is that practicing my faith plays a big part in helping me to enjoy the journey. Personally, I would find life empty if it was only all about me and my achievements. I know from experience that most professionals share a very similar view.

Living in the moment, being grateful and giving generously are all difficult. However, to me, these best practices for enjoying the journey are easy compared with believing in a God who has never been captured on film and doesn't have a social media presence. Faith has never been easy for me. I'm extremely analytical and struggle to believe in anything that can't be proven. Over the years I've done my best to "prove" that God exists beyond a reasonable doubt. I've read books on the subject (e.g. Lee Strobel), listened to hundreds of sermons and talked to a bunch of spiritual "experts." Each time, I reach the same conclusion: faith wouldn't mean a thing if it could be proven, that's why it's called faith.

Regardless of your view on the matter, there's one thing I know from experience: you'll find it easier to enjoy the journey if you believe that a supreme being/force/power other than yourself is calling the shots. If you're like me, and most of you are, faith in something that can't be seen, heard or quantitatively measured will be at times be extremely difficult. That's okay, I promise the struggle is worth the effort.

In the next and final chapter, I'm going to provide some powerful strategies for pushing through the resistance that professionals feel once they're challenged with a new way of living, especially when this approach is very different from the path you're currently traveling.

<u>Three Key Points to Remember</u>

1. None of what you've learned means a thing if you don't learn to enjoy the journey. This simple concept is made easier by following a handful of behaviors. The first of these is to learn from the past, prepare for the future but do your best to live exclusively in the moment.

2. The second strategy is to live gratefully. Seeing the glass as half full as opposed to half empty requires a simple, yet very difficult change in your perspective. However, this change makes an enormous difference in the way you enjoy your life.

3. Once you've developed a different outlook on how great you've got it, I recommend that you start focusing on giving to others. The data is clear, people who give of their resources (time and money) enjoy more satisfaction and happiness.

4. I know I promised three, but this one is far too important to skip. I've found (and research clearly supports) that a belief in a higher power can add significant meaning to your life. It's helpful to know that a being far wiser than any of us is calling the shots and has a plan that we could never intellectually comprehend.

Chapter 5 – Taking Action

You don't want to get to the very end of your life, make truckloads of money, out-achieve everyone you know and realize that you didn't enjoy the journey.

As an overachiever, taking the time to slow down and smell the roses isn't in your nature. You think that stopping to appreciate your hard work is for lazy people. This exercise is designed to get you focused on one of the strategies that's proven to add more satisfaction to your life: giving back to others. Here's how this works:

1. First, clarify your passions. One way to do this is to identify if there are any non-profits that have made a significant difference in your life.

2. Next, ask yourself what are the biggest challenges facing your community that resonate with you.

3. Identify one non-profit that could use your help. Once this is complete, contact this organization and offer to help financially or with your time. I highly recommend that you make a commitment to do this more than once. If you're struggling to find an organization to support, I recommend that you consider one of these resources:

    ◦ Charity Watch – www.CharityWatch.org

    ◦ Charity Navigator – www.CharityNavigator.org

    ◦ GuideStar – www.GuideStar.org

You can complete this exercise in the space below or by downloading a template at CoachCJ.com/bookexercises.

Non-Profits   Community Challenges

1   1

2   2

3   3

4   4

Organization	Commitment

CHAPTER 6

Momentum

"Take time to deliberate; but when the time for action arrives, stop thinking and go in."

— Andrew Jackson

I love the outdoors.

I enjoy the beauty and silence that only nature can provide. There are few things in this world that I appreciate doing more than going on a long hike with no real directions and simply absorbing the surroundings. I move slowly along a worn-out trail, listening quietly to the rustle of the trees or the occasional bird announcing its arrival.

Seven years ago, this passion for the outdoors led me to deliver an official proclamation to my entire family: It's time for me to become a "camper." This heartfelt declaration was met with absolute silence – no one believed I was serious. In an effort to demonstrate my commitment I made it absolutely clear that the only thing I wanted for my birthday (December 7) and Christmas was camping equipment.

And so, convinced that I would actually follow through on this latest obsession (unlike the Jack LaLanne Juicer that I used twice), I received the following camping supplies during the month of December 2010:

- Tent that sleeps six
- Two thermal sleeping bags (could handle the cold as low as ten degrees)
- Two halogen lamps
- Full stovetop set complete with propane tank
- Utensils for eating every meal imaginable
- Five-gallon jug for holding water
- Two air mattresses
- First aid kit
- Cast iron cooking set
- Waterproof matches
- Reinforced all-purpose tarp to place under the tent

Equipped with a more than adequate set of camping gear, I carefully planned a two-day camping excursion with my six-year-old son and my father-in-law. We set out on a chilly Friday afternoon to Shades State Park in central Indiana, where we had reserved a camping spot for the weekend. Shortly after arriving, we sat in lawn chairs, cracked open a couple of beers (juice box for Ian) and discussed the best way to get the gear set up. Two hours later, the tent was up, the mattress was inflated and a fire had been started to cook our gourmet meal of hot dogs and chips.

I remember sleeping about forty-seven minutes that night. I was cold, the mattress was uncomfortable and my father-in-law snored (a ton). The next morning I woke up with terrible pain in my lower back. I thought about taking a shower in the public facility to loosen up, but when I hobbled over there, I changed my mind: it was cold, damp and filthy. Less than an hour later, we packed up the gear (this wasn't easy – I was tempted to leave it) and I rushed home to take a hot shower, followed by a long nap in my own bed.

More than seven years later, all that gear sits in a gigantic blue tub in our garage –untouched. It turns out that while I do love the outdoors, I despise the effort required to set up and tear down all the equipment. In addition, I don't enjoy the idea of sleeping in the elements in a sleeping bag on a flimsy air mattress. But the part I despise the most is the idea of showering in a public facility that is cleaned about once every six months.

I'll be the first to admit that I'm a little soft.

Looking back, I can clearly see that the mistake I made was to get all excited, jump in head first and expect that my initial experience would be ideal. I was craving instant gratification and when I didn't get it, I quit. Now I'm the proud owner of hundreds of dollars of camping gear that gets referenced by my wife every time I want to try out a new hobby.

I'm 100% certain this story sounds familiar to you. Overachievers are easily seduced by something new that we can add to our ever-growing list of accomplishments. It doesn't matter if we're already overextended in every area of our lives, we presume there's just enough room for one more activity/hobby/ etc. But, as you know, 95% of the time we get distracted and quickly move on to something else.

Another great example of this takes place every time you

learn something new that you feel absolutely certain will make a positive difference in your life. We've all seen a documentary about healthy eating, attended a seminar reminding us of the power of compound interest, or read a great book on personal development, and thought, "Enough is enough, I've got to make a change!"

Unfortunately, approximately sixteen seconds after making this enthusiastic announcement, you make a decision that will crush your excitement and derail any momentum you might be feeling at the moment – you pick up your phone. The next thing you know, you've respond to eleven texts, five emails, taken a thirty-minute phone call and commented on a half dozen Facebook posts.

Sigh…

No matter how inspiring you found the documentary/seminar/book, its message is often quickly lost once you jump back into the "real world." Not only do you tend to forget what you learned, it's only a matter of days (maybe even hours) before you've moved on to the next big idea that promises to deliver immediate life-altering results.

Learning something new is easy, but changing behavior is extremely difficult. For this reason, I'm ending this journey with some simple advice to help you overcome the obstacles you will eventually run into along the way. These tactics will also help you generate momentum and become the type of person who actually enjoys all of their hard work and achievements.

Accountability

As I'm working this final chapter, it's early January of 2017.

That means a few things. It's cold, dark and rainy outside (lovely Indiana winters – but at least I'm not sleeping in a tent!) and my gym will be packed with tons of people who've made "getting into shape" their New Year's resolution. Instead of getting a spot right by the door, I now need to park a quarter mile from the entrance and get dressed in a locker room full of guys who think it's appropriate to blow dry their hair in the nude.

This minor inconvenience lasts until about the second week of February when most of these people quit showing up. This is good for me, but terrible for the person who desperately wants to start a healthier lifestyle. Selfishly, I enjoy the smaller crowd, but the coach in me is always frustrated by the lack of follow-through.

Throughout my career, the conversation frequently veers away from business and into the personal. When that happens, I'm asked, "How do I start an exercise routine?" hundreds, if not thousands of times. My answer is always the same. First, no matter what you do it's unlikely you'll ever be as fit as me, and second, you've got to create some accountability. I typically recommend one of the following ideas: hire a personal trainer – joining a gym isn't expensive enough to get you there on a regular basis – or get a workout partner; most people will follow through when they know someone is waiting on them to arrive.

This same advice applies to you and the information in this book. If you're truly committed to changing behavior, you'll need at the very least a little accountability. Here are a handful of tactics that I've seen work time and time again:

- *Hire a coach* – Coaching can be a very effective way to change behavior and achieve your goals. If you're skeptical about this approach, you should be. Coaching is a made-up industry that requires absolutely zero official education, training, or credentials. However, there are thousands of great coaches around the world who have a proven track record of making a massive difference in the lives of their clients. If you're not sure what kind of coach would be right for you, I would start by checking out what I believe is the most trusted resource in the industry: *International Coach Federation* (www.CoachFederation.org).

- *Get an Accountability Partner* – I've seen many people have great success by simply identifying a friend, peer, or family member who agrees to hold them accountable on a regular basis. The key to making this work is to select someone who you respect and know will be okay having the types of uncomfortable conversations that lead to change. In addition, this person should be able to deliver accountability without you taking it personally and getting upset. In other words, don't even think of asking your spouse.

- *Technology* – As of this writing there are approximately 3,456 apps (totally made-up number) that you can use to hold yourself accountable. They are great for setting up simple reminders that pop up on your calendar or send you an email. Personally, these don't work for me because I simply delete the reminder. However, I've had clients over the years discipline themselves to effectively use these tools.

- *ThriveMap University* – Based on the methods I have used to help hundreds of overachieving professionals meet their goals, I created this digital platform to inspire professionals just like you to make simple changes in their lives. In this powerful program, I've developed video tutorials, templates, quizzes and other resources that will help you to make meaningful change in your life. In addition, you'll be connected to a group of individuals who share your challenges. It's month-to-month, you can quit at any time and there's a no-questions-asked 100% money back guarantee. *To learn more, please visit www.ThriveMapU.com.*

Create a Trap

Let's assume for minute that you don't like the idea of being held accountable or it isn't convenient to have another person hold you responsible. In that case, I recommend that you consider creating a "trap." A trap is a consequence you design that will automatically take place if you don't follow through on your commitment.

The type of trap that is designed is different for everyone because we are all motivated by diverse consequences. In addition, the size and scope of your trap is directly related to the level of your commitment. In other words, if the goal isn't all that important, you'll design a consequence that is fairly insignificant. The following examples will help you understand this concept:

- *Exercise* – As I mentioned above, for some people signing up for a race can be a good trap, especially if you challenge someone else to sign up and maybe even wager on who will complete with a better time. This works especially well for men whose egos rarely allow them to let someone else to win at anything, at least without a really good fight.

- *Family Commitment* – I once had a client tell me that he wanted to take his family to Disney World but couldn't find the time or the money to make it happen. I challenged him to pick a day in the future (in his case, one year out) and tell his kids they were going. I knew those kids would never let him wiggle out of it, and I was right. About fourteen months later, he and his family had the vacation of a lifetime. The trap didn't make finding the money and time easier, it just made it more important.

- *Charity* - Many years ago, I agreed to give all of the proceeds from an event I was hosting to a local non-profit. I did a poor job of marketing the program and had about twenty people signed up less than six weeks out. I decided to pick up the phone and guarantee the organization $10,000 no matter how many people attended. Knowing that I might have to write a check for $10,000 out of my own pocket motivated me to fill the room.

- *Home Improvement* – Imagine that you've wanted to finish your basement for years, but can never seem to make it a priority. Go ahead and invite your extended family (including seven kids under the age of nine) to Thanksgiving dinner next year. The visual of seven kids wrestling in your living room for eight-to-ten hours is the best motivation to start getting quotes from contractors.

Like personal accountability, the exact trap you choose is irrelevant. What matters is that it motivates you to actually change behavior.

Be Patient

Many years ago, I was helping my then girlfriend (now wife) move from one apartment to another. As I'm sure you're well aware, moving is awful. It involves tons of trips in and out of box trucks, navigating furniture through small doors, and a decent amount of body odor. I would probably rather have an appendicitis than ever move again.

But I was in love and would do whatever this young woman asked of me. Still, I hated the exercise. I wanted it to be over as quickly as possible. I rushed in and out of her apartment, often asking, "Can't we just throw this away?" I paid very little attention to what I was doing, and received the "Slow down and be careful!" warning about every seven minutes.

Dismissing this advice, I picked up a small dresser and made my way to the moving van. Unfortunately, in my haste I failed to notice that the drawers had yet to be removed. Seconds after picking up the dresser, one of the drawers – a very heavy piece of wood – fell out and landed on my big toe. I screamed, uttered every curse word I had ever learned, and sat on the front step hoping the pain would go away. After a few minutes, I decided it was prudent to take off my shoe and look at the damage. I didn't even need to see the toe because my sock was full of blood. I rushed off to the emergency room and received five stitches in what the doctor admitted was probably the most sensitive part of the entire body.

I've been told on more than one occasion that I may have a small problem with patience. Unless you're the one easy-going laid-back overachiever on the planet, you can empathize with this challenge. You don't like waiting any more than I do. You roll your eyes at the checkout line when someone reaches for coupons, honk at the car in front of you .5 seconds after the light turns green, and assume you're being ignored if your text isn't returned immediately.

Patience is one of the most challenging characteristics for a driven individual to acquire. Trust me, I know from years of experience working at it. Despite the difficulty, it's important that you recognize no matter how brilliant this advice may seem, you will not have a significant transformation in your behavior overnight. You've been doing it your way for a long time and meaningful change rarely happens quickly.

That's the bad news.

The good news is that I am 100% confident you can discipline yourself to patiently work through this process and see a measurable difference in your quality of life. Here's a handful of strategies to help get you going:

- *Set Clear Expectations* – As you begin this process and consider involving others in your plans or building traps, recognize that this journey will never end – you will always be a work in progress. The world is going to keep reinforcing the broken definition of success (work a ton, earn recognition, money and acquisitions, then repeat) and you will feel the temptation to jump back on the treadmill. Resist this urge and recognize the long game.

- *Eat the Elephant* – You know the best way to eat an elephant – one bite at a time. Even though the process of transformation I outline is uncomplicated, you will struggle if you try to work on too many things at once. You can set aside a morning to identify your unique talents, decide which relationships are most important and set some killer goals – but I would advise against it. Quick and rushed effort leads to crappy results. Take it one step at a time and you will be more likely to succeed.

- *Reflect* – The overachiever in you is going to want to measure results immediately and is probably frustrated that I didn't provide a checklist in this book. As you move through this journey, I encourage you to frequently pause and think about what you're learning about yourself. The truth is that while your growth won't be easy to put into a spreadsheet, it will be meaningful and will have a huge impact in your life. Unfortunately, unless you reflect, you may not "feel" like you're making as much progress as you'd like.

- *Remember* - "All good things come to those who wait."

Pick Up the Baton

Imagine for a minute that you're attending the summer Olympics. It's a beautiful sunny day and you're sitting in the track and field stadium with a handful of your closest friends. You've had a few beers and you're getting ready to watch the finals of the women's 4x100 relay. There's no doubt about who will win the gold – the United States is the hands down favorite. The only question is whether or not they will set a new World's Record.

The gun sounds and seven amazing athletes burst from the starting blocks. Before the baton is handed off for the first exchange, the U.S. team has a commanding lead. The lead grows as the race progresses and the split times indicate that the World Record is within reach.

As the anchor for the U.S. prepares to complete the final leg of the race, you almost ignore the huge lead, focusing exclusively on the number they need to hit to make history.

Then the unthinkable happens. Something goes wrong with the handoff and the baton falls onto the track. The World Record is lost. The last runner rolls her eyes towards the sky, clearly furious with herself and no doubt wondering how she made such an enormous mistake. As the other runners are catching up, what are you screaming at the top of your lungs?

"Pick up the baton!!"

I want you to remember this story every time you screw up. Why? Because stopping to beat yourself up over a past mistake adds absolutely zero value. Quickly learn your lesson and move on, because the race isn't going to stop and wait for you.

My message has reached thousands of people over the years and during that time I have never received the following email:

Dear CJ,

Thanks so much for your inspiring words. I followed your advice exactly as prescribed and have achieved the exact results you promised. In addition, I didn't have any setbacks or unforeseen obstacles along the way. I simply committed to a change in behavior, executed flawlessly and moved on to the next step in the process.

I'm fully aware that the information presented in this short book is easy to understand. In fact, it may seem so simple and straightforward that you can't imagine *not* making these changes in your life.

Nevertheless, as I've mentioned, there's a HUGE gap between knowing what to do and doing it. Experience tells me that no matter how disciplined you may be, you will stumble more than a few times on this journey. When this happens, you'll be tempted to beat yourself up, wondering, *How could I possibly fail to follow through on something this simple?*

If there was any value in this "I'm such an idiot" exercise, I would recommend that you sit down with your journal after every mistake and carefully document the many reasons that you're incompetent.

The truth is that there really is "no use in crying over spilled milk." Life is full of mistakes, failure and lack of follow through. Meaningful growth rarely comes from doing everything right the first time, or, as Bill Gates pointed out, *"Success is a lousy teacher."*[xxiv]

Cut yourself some slack. If this type of change were easy, no one would ever feel overwhelmed, anxious or frustrated. When you stumble, which you will, my advice is simple: Pick up the baton and get back into the race.

It's Time for Action

Your time is extremely valuable. You could have watched a movie, gone to the gym, or put in a few more hours at the office,

---

xxiv Justin Bryant, "Success Is A Lousy Teacher. It Seduces Smart People Into Thinking They Can't Lose," Self Made Success, May 27, 2016, http://selfmadesuccess.com/success-is-a-lousy-teacher-it-seduces-smart-people/.

but instead, you gave this book a quick read and allowed me to be a part of your journey. For that, I am extremely grateful.

I'm tempted to wish you "good luck" on this journey, but the truth is that luck has almost nothing to do with your ability to execute what you've learned in these pages. It's up to you, and my experience working with professionals for more than thirteen years tells me that you're more than up to the task. Now, it's time for action.

<u>Three Key Points to Remember</u>

1. You have now completed yet another "personal development" resource (book, podcast, retreat, etc.) – congratulations. Unfortunately, learning something new doesn't mean squat if you don't change your behavior. The best way to ensure that you actually practice what you've learned is to employ one of these two simple tactics.

   ○ *Accountability* – Consider involving someone else on your journey (friend, coach or personal trainer, etc.) because almost no one has the ability to hold themselves accountable.

   ○ *Set a Trap* – In those instances where working with someone else doesn't make sense, build a "trap" which delivers a consequence if you don't follow through on your commitment.

2. The advice in this short book is extremely simple and straight-forward. However, no matter what your brain is telling you at this very moment, change will not happen overnight. That's not the way it works. Remember, this is a journey not a quick exercise that you can complete in a couple of hours and then check it off as "complete." Be patient.

3. I've delivered this message to thousands of people over the years. Not one has successfully implemented everything without a setback. When you stumble, which you will, pick yourself up and keep moving – there's absolutely zero value in beating yourself up.

Chapter 6 – Taking Action

Now that we've reached the end, I think it's time to let you in on a little secret. Personal development, self-help books don't work. These are just words on a piece of paper – it's what you do with them that matters. In this final exercise, I challenge you create the types of simple traps necessary to make meaningful progress towards your most important goals.

Here's how this works:

1. In the first column list at least three objectives that you'd like to accomplish in the next twelve months. These are probably goals that you've struggled to achieve in the past.

2. In the second column list a trap that's powerful enough to help hold you accountable.

You can complete this exercise in the space below or by downloading a template at CoachCJ.com/bookexercises.

Goal/Objective	Trap
Salesperson exceeding their annual quota so they can earn more than $100k which would allow them to take their family on a great summer vacation.	Book a trip to Disney World and tell the kids about it.

	Goal/Objective	Trap
1		
2		
3		
4		
5		

Bibliography

Alcocer, Paulina. "History of Standardized Testing in the United States." NEA. Accessed March 15, 2017. http://www.nea.org/home/66139.htm.

Belfort, Jordan. *The Wolf of Wall Street*. New York: Bantam, 2007.

Bryant, Justin. "Success Is A Lousy Teacher. It Seduces Smart People Into Thinking They Can't Lose." Self Made Success. May 27, 2016. Accessed March 15, 2017. http://selfmadesuccess.com/success-is-a-lousy-teacher-it-seduces-smart-people/.

Carpenter, Dave. Cartoon. Cartoon Stock. https://www.cartoonstock.com/directory/k/karat.asp.

Csikszentmihalyi, Mihaly. *Flow: the Psychology of Optimal Experience*. New York: Harper Perennial Modern Classics, 2008.

"Examples of Skills." YourDictionary. Accessed March 15, 2017. http://examples.yourdictionary.com/examples-of-skills.html.

Fletcher, Dan. "Standardized Testing." Time. December 11, 2009. Accessed March 15, 2017. http://content.time.com/time/nation/article/0,8599,1947019,00.htm.

Gilbert, Daniel. *Stumbling on Happiness*. New York: Vintage Books, 2007.

Gregson, Jonathan. "The Richest Countries in the World." Global Finance Magazine. February 13, 2017. Accessed March 13, 2017. https://www.gfmag.com/global-data/economic-data/richest-countries-in-the-world?page=12.

Hinojosa, Maria. "On September 11, final words of love." CNN. September 10, 2002. Accessed March 15, 2017. http://edition.cnn.com/2002/US/09/03/ar911.phone.calls/.

"Hunger and Poverty Facts and Statistics." Feeding America. Accessed March 15, 2017. http://www.feedingamerica.org/hunger-in-america/impact-of-hunger/hunger-and-poverty/hunger-and-poverty-fact-sheet.html.

Lencioni, Patrick. "If everything is important…" The Table Group. March 2006. Accessed March 13, 2017. https://www.tablegroup.com/blog/if-everything-is-important.

Lieber, Ron. "Why You Should Tell Your Kids How Much You Make." *New York Times*, February 1, 2015.

Lindstrom, Martin. *Buyology: Truth and Lies About Why We Buy*. New York: Broadway Books, 2010.

"List of state achievement tests in the United States." Wikipedia. Last modified March 03, 2017. Accessed March 15, 2017. https://en.wikipedia.org/wiki/List_of_state_achievement_tests_in_the_United_States.

Mays, Elizabeth. "Aristotle on Education." New Foundations. Last modified April 30, 2014. http://www.newfoundations. com/GALLERY/Aristotle.html.

"Melody Beattie Quotes." Goodreads. Accessed March 13, 2017. https://www.goodreads.com/author/quotes/4482.Melody_ Beattie.

"Mirrorgrams." Altoona Mirror, December 13, 1944.

"No Child Left Behind Act." Wikipedia. Last modified March 11, 2017. Accessed March 15, 2017. https://en.wikipedia. org/wiki/No_Child_Left_Behind_Act#Replacement.

Noonan, Peggy. "The Sounds That Still Echo From 9/11." *The Wall Street Journal*, September 9, 2006. https://www.wsj. com/articles/SB115774704992357920.

Plochmann, G. K. *Plato*. New York: Dell Publishing Company, 1973.

"Taylor Protocols - The Core Values Index." Taylor Protocols. Accessed March 13, 2017. https://www.taylorprotocols.com/ CVI.php.

Tyack, David. "Ways of Seeing: An Essay on the History of Compulsory Schooling." *Harvard Educational Review* 46, no. 3 (1976): 355-89. doi: 10.17763/ haer.46.3.v73405527200106v.

About the Author

CJ McClanahan is a business coach, speaker and author who specializes in helping Type A professionals shift from simply chasing success to actually enjoying all their hard work. After beginning his career with Arthur Andersen, he shifted his focus towards small business. His next executive role included responsibility for managing operations, finance and IT. His last corporate position provided him with the opportunity to manage a large sales team in the software industry.

In 2003, five days before the birth of his first child, CJ quit his job, took all his savings and started a small coaching firm. Over the last fourteen years, he has worked with hundreds of talented executives, helping them achieve record sales and profits. In addition, he's developed a proven system for helping them get off the treadmill and reassess their priorities while continuing to grow their professional careers.

CJ lives in Fishers, IN with his amazing wife Nicole and their two children.

CPSIA information can be obtained
at www.ICGtesting.com
Printed in the USA
BVOW03s2047300617
488271BV00001B/41/P